*For Elsie Luxton and Joyce Taylor*

# RETURN TO AKENFIELD

*Portrait of an English Village in the
21st Century*

## CRAIG TAYLOR

**Granta Books**
London

Granta Publications, 2/3 Hanover Yard, London N1 8BE

First published in Great Britain by Granta Books, 2006
This edition published by Granta Books, 2007

A CIP catalogue record for this book is available from
the British Library.

1 3 5 7 9 10 8 6 4 2

Typeset by M Rules
Printed and bound in Great Britain by
Bookmarque Ltd, Croydon, Surrey

**Craig Taylor** is a journalist and playwright. He writes for the *Guardian* and has written for the *New York Times Magazine* and *McSweeney's*. Some of his 'One Million Tiny Plays about London' have been staged at the Hampstead Theatre. He lives in London.

# CONTENTS

On a recent flight from London to Vancouver, I decided against buying a set of headphones for the in-flight entertainment. I missed the romantic comedy and the historical drama and, with my window shade down, even a glimpse of the glaciers of Greenland. But when the plane began its descent into Calgary for a short stopover I slid the shade up and there was a spectacular view of the brown squares of prairies below. After spending the last few months interviewing residents and farmers in a small Suffolk village, I still had the English landscape fresh in my mind. The sight below was a shock. The land seemed to be faked, it was so uniform. I had seen the prairies before, from the ground and from the air, but I hadn't remembered quite how perfect the land was for farming. The soil 37,000 feet below this plane didn't change for hundreds of kilometres; the soil around the Suffolk village I had been living in differed from one side of the A12 to the other. The long squares of this flat land were cut through by ruler-straight roads, and the farms stretched on for days; they had none of the dips, valleys, or clingy Iocene clay of the Suffolk countryside. I was reminded of the words of one of the farmers I spoke to while conducting interviews for this book. It was a brief comment, given sometime when the recorder was turned off and I was stuffing the equipment into my bag. 'If you were to choose anywhere in the world to put agriculture,' he said, 'you wouldn't choose to put it in England.'

In our globalized world of agribusiness and food miles, Suffolk's sloping fields and dense hedgerows can seem hopelessly archaic compared to the prairies. I came out to the Suffolk countryside to find out how life in a village had changed in the last thirty-five years, and how agriculture was changing with it. The land has its own appeal, most famously celebrated in a book called *Akenfield* by Ronald Blythe.

*Akenfield*, published in 1969, is a rich and perceptive portrait of life in an English village, told in the voices of the farmers and villagers themselves. Blythe, who had published fiction and a work of social history and had edited editions of Austen, Hardy and Hazlitt for the Penguin Classics series, spent the winter of 1966–7 in what he called 'a kind of natural conversation with three generations' of his Suffolk neighbours, teasing out their thoughts on 'farming, education, welfare, class, religion and indeed life and death'. The bestselling book that resulted captured their lives and the nature of rural life in England at a time of great change. *Akenfield* has remained in print ever since, been translated into more than twenty languages and inspired an elegiac, fictionalized film by another Suffolk man, Sir Peter Hall. 'My only real credentials,' Blythe wrote later, 'were that I was native to its situation in nearly every way and had only to listen to hear my own world talking.'

The world that did the talking was vivid in the detail it accorded everyday tasks and poignant in its evocation of a disappearing past. The farm worker remembered the horrors and adventure of Gallipoli before returning to the routine life of the farm; the blacksmith described forging his own nails; the thatcher recounted his pleasure in the look of a finished roof where 'the reeds shine silver and grey, and the deep eaves are cut razor sharp'.

At a time when farmers were becoming more like 'agricultural technicians', the farm workers in *Akenfield* described their connection to the old clay of Suffolk's soil – how they coaxed it, marked it, ploughed it, cursed it and occasionally questioned its worth altogether – and revealed stores of knowledge that technological progress was beginning to erase. 'Science is a footnote to what the countryman really believes,' Blythe wrote. 'And what he knows is often incommunicable.'

But *Akenfield* did not bow to sentimental ideas of the countryside as idyll. Blythe's villagers spoke too of the brutality of country life, and of hopes to escape the village. Their lives were a complex mix of wide-open spaces and limited opportunities. As Blythe later remarked, 'I think my view of human life is how brief and curious most people's lives are. Yet when you come to talk to them you realize how strong they are and how unbelievably rich their lives are; also subtle and various.'

Western Canada, where I grew up, is thousands of miles from Suffolk. But like so many readers I was taken by the vividness of Blythe's book and the way it prised open this far-off world, a place with its own songs, its own traditions of planting and harvest, and even its own breed of horse. In 2004, living in London and re-reading *Akenfield*, I wondered what the lives of those who lived and worked in Akenfield now were like, and how much had changed – or remained the same – in the generation since the book was published. So around harvest time, I took two trains and a taxi to the two neighbouring Suffolk villages Blythe had renamed Akenfield. I rented a room in Blythe's old house, which is now a bed and breakfast with a stack of boardgames in the sitting room and a sturdy three-speed bike in the shed. I cycled around, often turning off my headlight at night, when the fields were bright with moonlight.

Akenfield now is in many ways still as Blythe described it:

The village lies folded away in one of the shallow valleys which dip into the East Anglian coastal plain. It is not a particularly striking place and says little at first meeting. It is approached by a spidery lane running off from the 'bit of straight', as they call it, meaning a handsome stretch of Roman road, apparently going nowhere . . . It is the kind of road which hurries one past a situation. Centuries of traffic must have passed within yards of Akenfield without noticing it.

That bit of straight is now a road where no pedestrians are welcome. The B1078 is never covered by a steady stream of traffic, but every few minutes a car roars past. There are rabbits, voles, ferrets all ground down to bumps on the road by those making their hastened journeys, no more noticeable than the rush of fields outside the car window. People used to miss Akenfield because of disinterest. Now, they miss it because of speed.

There is still livestock in Akenfield but it only reveals itself when the wind changes course. Occasionally the smell of ducks comes in from the duck farm, as well as the sound of an odd, frantic quack. When the wind turns at the other end of the village, by the garage, it carries the smell from the pig farm and an occasional squeal. There's evidence of the few cows left in the puddles on the roads heading to Dallinghoo.

On most autumn days the Suffolk wind blows in hard and does its work leaving the breeze to dislodge the rest of the leaves from the ash trees. Occasionally, off the B1078, the only sound is the light slap of falling leaves on the outside corner of the wheat field, where the turns of the drilling tractors have left the soil softly curved as if shaped by a butterknife.

The village lies in a valley, etched out, ancient and circular, surrounded by orchards and fields, and deep enough that for some reason no mobile phone company other than Vodafone seems to get decent reception at its centre. When it gets dark at night and the sodium lights of the school and the street lamps near the pub are obscured, the Norman steeple of the church stands against the dark sky just as it would have centuries ago.

But some changes were obvious. There has been a noticeable increase in the population: according to Blythe's book, after a steady decline through the middle of the twentieth century, there were 298 people living in Akenfield in 1961; the 2001 census lists 358. The two shops and the post office mentioned in *Akenfield* are gone, converted to private houses, and the vicarage sits empty behind disused tennis courts. A street built in 1976 to house British Telecom workers at their new research centre in Martlesham wouldn't look out of place in any London commuter town. On the back of the cutlery in the pub's bright dining room is that telltale sign of contemporary life: IKEA. And just a few days before I arrived, the village was wired for broadband Internet access.

Other changes became apparent as I sought out people who had appeared in *Akenfield*. All of the villagers who worked in the old professions – the wheelwright, the saddler, the blacksmith – are dead, and most of their professions have gone with them. Others have moved on: the assistant teacher became the headteacher and retired to a nearby town; the farm student became a farmer elsewhere. In their places now are commuters and entrepreneurs and retirees from other parts of the country. The family names in the local graveyard are no longer the surnames of the people living in the houses.

The broad Suffolk accent caught in Akenfield is more muted too. The language of the 'old boys' is full of mischievous *o*s that sneak into words normally without them. But the families moving into the village speak in the 'Estuarine' accent (the estuary being the Thames) that has spread throughout southern England or in what used to be called BBC English. The occasional word still rings with a hint of Suffolk. The headteacher told me she was a little worried when she heard her young son say the word *compoo-ah*.

*Akenfield* appeared at a time of enormous changes in British agriculture. The hum of the large combines in the fields was still new to some; fewer labourers were needed to bring in the crops, making farm jobs more contingent and less secure. The power relationship between farmer and farm worker was shifting towards equality, as they were increasingly the only two people working in the field. All of these changes have continued. Farming now is a story of amalgamation, of increasing specialization, of slow decline and tenacity in the face of supermarket rationalization, foreign competition and government regulation.

Blythe himself now lives an hour away from Akenfield, near Colchester, in a small cottage. The people of his old village have not forgotten him. A hardcover copy of *Akenfield* sits on the side table at the bed and breakfast and the building company in the village is now named after it. Over several months I interviewed him and about fifty of Akenfield's current residents. Some of what they had to say appears in the pages that follow.

Once, when I was speaking with Blythe in front of his fireplace, he paused and looked out of the window. 'Imagine what the farmers who lived here would think of this,' he said. 'Us doing nothing but talk all afternoon.'

*Prologue*

## RONALD BLYTHE
### WRITER, 83

*He has well-combed white hair, a small, curving smile and a*
*patient voice. He lives alone in an ancient, low-beamed cottage*
*that once belonged to the painter John Nash. We walk around*
*the edges of local fields and occasionally in a show of spry fitness,*
*he jumps a ditch as we talk.*

I was born in Acton in 1922. It's a typical Suffolk village between Lavenham and Sudbury, in west Suffolk. My parents and grandparents lived there, but we moved away when I was small. Well, only about two miles away. That first house had a thatched roof and pond and pigsty; it was an ancient East Anglian house made of beams and thatch. It burnt down after the last war, so I used to see this great chimney standing up in the garden when I passed on my way to Bury St Edmunds. Now it's just got three modern bungalows on the site.

I'm the eldest of six, country children. We walked and bicycled everywhere and knew the whole place for miles around. It was during the time of the great agricultural depression, which started in the late nineteenth century and then bucked up because of the First World War, when agriculture was subsidized. Then the subsidies were taken off, so we were brought up in a kind of beautiful, ruinous landscape of great rural poverty. But we didn't know it, because the fields were full of wild flowers.

My father was at Gallipoli, a young man off a Suffolk farm in his teens. He was a very gentle, kind and rather silent man who loved animals, especially horses. Suffolk had the punches that pulled the ploughs, the biggest horses in Europe, and my father was a great horseman. I've got snapshots somewhere of him in the Middle East during the First World War, on a horse near the Pyramids. He was what was called a dispatch rider: he'd take messages on the horse. Farm workers weren't called up until 1917 – they were meant to grow as much food as they could – but my father went in 1914. He was glad to go. It was such a romantic thing. Country boys like him had never been abroad and they all thought that it was wonderful to get off the land in those days. He went on a great liner called the *Aquitania* to Gallipoli and was not hurt at all, right through the war. He came back and worked on a farm as a stockman, looking after all the animals.

My mother came from London and was well read, a different kind of person altogether. She loved the country. She didn't like London; she repudiated it, really. One of the things I remember most from my childhood is going for walks with her and telling her lies about the distance. 'No, it's only a little ways further,' I would tell her. And we'd walk and walk.

I was a great watcher and listener, an explorer. I loved history and looking at old churches. I was very much a country boy of that period, the kind that hardly exists now. One of the things I think is sad these days is this business where people think children are going to be molested all the time. They're all cooped up with their computers. But when we were children we were outside. You couldn't go anywhere without seeing boys in the summertime in the river or walking or playing football or just wandering about on their bikes. The countryside was full of children, it seemed. It was the last scrap, I suppose, of that old life.

In every country there are indigenous writers who are made by landscape. The great ones, of course, are Thomas Hardy and John Clare and to a degree Wordsworth, but in every country there are people who haven't gone far and have drawn everything they know and understand from quite a small place. I think that might have happened to me, but without my knowing it. My knowledge was extended by reading widely and in other languages – that made a lot of difference – but on the whole I think that I was made by this place.

My two or three greatest friends were botanists, including John Nash, the painter. I learned from them about plants and ecology and the climate. Later I discovered all sorts of things about architecture; East Anglia is full of the most wonderful buildings from the Middle Ages. I suppose I lived very much in the world into which I was born, but with a wider culture. I was really brought up by artists. They all lived in the middle of nowhere and painted. First there was Sir Cedric Morris. He and his friend Lett Haines, who taught Lucian Freud, had come to Suffolk in the mid-1930s and set up the East Anglian School of Painting and Drawing at Hadleigh. It was like a little bit of France in the middle of Suffolk, because the house was painted blue and it always smelt of garlic and wine. All sorts of people were taught how to paint there, in the old-fashioned way without classes and exams.

I was working as a reference librarian at Colchester when I met a charming woman named Christine Nash. She had married John Nash, who had been an official war artist and had come to live on the Suffolk–Essex border. In the midst of all these painters, Christine knew perfectly well I should be a writer, and told me so. Somehow she got me out of the job at the library, to my mother's anxiety, and she found me a little house on the Suffolk coast. Later I was introduced to Benjamin Britten and he gave me a job writing and editing the programme book for the Aldeburgh Festival and all sorts of little literary things. I stayed there two years and wrote my first book, a novel set by the sea. And then, in 1960, I went off and to my own amazement found a little house by myself, near the village I called Akenfield. It was the first time I had ever done anything sensible, really.

One day a few years later, Penguin in London and Pantheon in New York contacted me. Village life was changing all over the world, they said, and they wanted to do a series of books about it together. They would send a Russian writer to the French countryside or a French writer to Russia, that sort of thing. Mostly the books were to be written by sociologists. When they came to me and said that I should do one about Britain, I told them I was not a sociologist remotely, nor had I heard of the term oral history at the time. Besides, I'd seen outside the window of this house all my life. What was interesting about it? But I agreed to do it. I thought to do something unusual.

I did vaguely think about doing it in Wales, where I had some friends, because it was so different and stimulating. But I couldn't get started. I was editing Hazlitt at the time for Penguin and I quite liked this bookish thing, working in libraries and being scholarly. They said, 'Have you started this book yet?' So I went for a walk around Akenfield. It was an awful February day. The ditches were full of churning water coming through the field drains. These were partly the medieval ditches of the village. When I looked down I could see what people had seen for centuries: that is, a limited place of seasonal toil. I went to speak to the village nurse. Although I knew her very well, I soon realized I didn't know her at all. Once she started speaking about her own life, another person emerged. When I got home, I was astonished, shaken really, by knowing what I now knew about her. I wrote it down and that other person emerged: she worked in what was really an army hut, she'd got a club foot (which I never put in the book because I thought it would upset her), she delivered all the children and laid out all the dead and patched people up with basically Vaseline and strips of sheets. It was a terrible time she was in, full of hardship.

From there, I just shaped the book. I cycled around on a Raleigh, which I've still got. I would ask somebody to talk to me about keeping pigs – and suddenly he would tell me something astonishing about himself, or be so open about his emotional life that I was astounded. Often I hardly asked any questions at all, I just listened. These were people whose lives covered the 1880s to the 1960s, and they talked about bell-ringing and ploughing and the church and the village school.

Akenfield could be anywhere. It's not spectacular; it's just an ordinary farming community with much the same history as hundreds of villages in this part of the world. They started out as Saxon communities with one or two fields, usually with moorland or woodland all around them, and they just spread out over the centuries. They have medieval churches and sometimes a Baptist chapel, and the pub of course. So the book was meant to be about not a special village but any village. At the time we had no idea these professions wouldn't last for ever. There used to be a joke when we were at school: 'Forward, men of the Middle Ages!' But then there was a sense of things changing. The book was just a pattern of the world into which I was born.

*Farming I: 'That's a Lovely Apple'*

*He is in his sitting room, before a crackling fire, reading short humorous stories printed by the Farmer's Press. There is a selection of fresh apples in the basket by his easy chair. He is soft-spoken but belongs to the local Amateur Dramatic Society, and over the years he has brought to life some major roles at the village hall, including Jack in* Jack and the Beanstalk.

I was born in 1947, just up the road. Before you get to the farm there are two cottages on the left-hand side; I was born in the one on the left. When I got married I moved down the road. I'm still here.

My father lost his dad quite early, so he had to work to keep money coming in for his mother and sister. He started on the farm when he was fifteen and spent all his life there. It must have been about 1980 when I took over as foreman from him. He retired and I just slotted in. The first day weren't as bad as I thought it was going to be, as they were all great men what worked there. There was eighteen men working on the farm full-time. Now there's three. There's hardly anybody there these days.

I didn't have much to do with the agricultural side, the arable side of it, which is now all done under contract anyway. I was just foreman over the fruit. There used to be 140 acres of apples and pears. Now I reckon we've got about twenty-five acres of them: fifteen acres of Coxes, six or seven acres of Bramleys, some James Grieves and about five acres of Conference pears. That's all the apples and pears we've got left now. We've also got five acres of plums, about 100 acres of blackcurrants and the rest are made up of sugar beets, sweetcorn, that sort of thing.

All our Bramleys go for what we call peeling. They're peeled and put into Mr Kipling pies and things like that. For the peeling machine you have to have an apple between seventy and 100 millimetres; anything over that is too big. The peeling machine won't take it, so you just can't sell the big apples. This year we've had wet weather and the apples were just exploding. Big, beautiful apples. All those will be thrown away. When the ladies pick them off the tree they sort them in the boxes. That's how they're graded. The small ones that are sent away go in one box and the big ones go in another box. We've still got about a dozen bins of over-size. Sometimes we'll sell the over-size, sometimes we won't. You work all year pruning the trees, spraying the trees and then you just see them all wasted.

For the last few years we've had some organic apples. You don't spray those trees for three years before you can sell them as organic but you still spray them with a sulphur. People think organic stuff is not sprayed at all, but it is. The sulphur's supposed to keep all the bugs away but it don't. The results are terrible, the trees are dying. You just have to sell it for juice.

All the apples the supermarkets want now are Coxes and Bramleys. We used to have Worcesters and they were lovely and sweet, a real tasting apple. It was a lot redder than Coxes or Bramleys, it was red all round. We used to have George Caves, Scarlet Pimpernels, Laxton's, but we haven't got them any more. The Coxes have size restrictions too. We don't pick Coxes over eighty millimetres to sell in the supermarkets. You don't see apples like that in the supermarket because they don't sell them.

I suppose they think, A child wouldn't eat a big apple, would they? Well, we had one between us last night, me and the wife. It was lovely.

The supermarkets don't sell them small and they don't sell them big. The apples have to be a perfect size and they have to be a perfect colour too. For a Cox it has to have about 25 per cent flush colour. Anything greener is not picked. They need the colour and they need the proper size to sell in a supermarket, or so they say. If they see it's got a mark it will have to go on the floor. But look at this big Cox. That's a lovely apple, isn't it?

Years ago, they used to pick everything. The orchard was picked clean, and they used to pick the ones up off the floor – those were used for cider. But no one wants them now.

I think in years to come the English apple will be gone. So far this year we've cut down five acres of them, and we're cutting another eight down, so we'll have cut down over ten again this year. There was a lady walking through the orchard the other day. There's one or two public footpaths that go through and this lady walks every day right by the fruit shed. 'I love this walk with all these trees this time of the year,' she said to me. 'They begin to change colour. What are you doing cutting them down?' She said she didn't want the landscape to change. I told her that I'm sorry to see it go as much as her. It's just that it's my livelihood and I've got another eight years to go until retirement.

We get rid of the orchard tree by tree. We cut the apple tree down with a power saw and dig it out with a digger. We save the wood because the farmer's got wood burners at home, so he burns it on the fire. We push all the other stuff in a big heap and burn it, just plough it up and there you are. We had some Worcesters up to this year but we just cut those down. I've got some Worcester wood stacked in my garden. I burn the trees at home as well. That's what's on the fire right now. We get two warms out of it, you see: we get a nice warm as we're cutting it down and we get a warm as it burns.

The ones we've cut down this year are trees that were put in in 1956, almost the oldest. For a long time a man named Bernard Catchpole worked here with my father, and he kept all the records. He used to put everything down in his diary. My dad and Bernard were here the other day, and I asked my dad when some of them were planted. He said, 'That was the year Jack Kindred started, but I can't remember what year that was. I'll ask Bernard.' So Bernard got his little book out – 1956, right there on the page.

Up to eight to ten years ago, we used to have about fifty apple pickers. Now we're down to about twenty. There's just not so many trees to pick. We've got the same ones that come every year. I've got their telephone numbers and I ring up and say, 'Do you want a job apple picking?' Oh yeah, yeah. We get a lot of students that come. I put up little postcards – APPLE PICKERS NEEDED – all hand-done, good rates of pay.

We've got one family, Liverpudlians, that have been coming every year for fifteen or twenty years. There's Old Mum, we call her, she's got seven or eight children, all grown up, who come down from Liverpool and help to pick apples. They just love it. They don't need the money but there are those who do. We used to have some from Ipswich, local people. I suppose the ones who need the money most are the students who are at university, just a job for the summertime.

Every year you'll get beginners. Some are all right but some never will learn. They're a lot brainier than what I am, but to pick an apple they're hopeless. It frustrates me because I've picked apples all my life. I just put the bucket under and get on with it. They'll pick an apple off the tree and they'll stand and look at it and they turn it and 'Yes, that's all right' and they put it in the bucket one at a time. It's so frustrating watching them. You have to say something . . . 'Come on, get a move on.' We'll probably get rid of one or two during the course of the season. You have to. They never will learn. You don't need to look at every apple! Most of them look the same.

We have had some people from other countries. They come and done some pruning for us last year. Russian, I think. It was a country near Russia, beginning with an A. But, my God, do they work. They don't stop. There's not one of them who can speak English, but we had an interpreter come for about an hour and you have to make hand signals to how to prune a tree. The interpreter was one of them. This is sort of a gang, they have people come in, they live in their houses and send them out to work on the farms. You don't pay the people what come to work, you pay the person they're employed by.

But most of the year it's just the three of us. We work together quite well really. I've been working with them most of our lives. There's two Philips who have been working on the farm. One is on the fruit side and one works with the contracting firm most of the while, but when he's not he works with us. So he's actually got two bosses. We all get on quite well. We talk to each other about this and that. Football, Ipswich Town – I used to go quite regular. I used to go because my boy liked football and I used to take him. There's too much money in football now, isn't there? They get too much wages. These players could buy a blackcurrant machine every match.

My dad loves his apples. He comes over and picks his apples even now. He doesn't like to see them left on the trees because, you see, in his time we didn't leave them on the trees. He lives in a sheltered accommodation nearby, looks after himself during the week pretty well. He's learned to cook. He comes in his car to get his apples.

He says to me the other day, 'I was thinking about coming over and getting me some more Bramleys.'

I said, 'Well, I'll get you some if you like, Dad, and I'll bring them down when I see you.'

'No, no, no, I love coming,' he says, 'I'll come and get them.'

He's eighty-nine. It does him good to be out with the trees. He wears his old cap — not his overalls but his old coat — and he still knows how to pick an apple properly. The other week, he was making a list of all the apples and plums he knew. I think he's got over thirty different sorts of apples he could think of.

When we take down the apple trees we'll replace them with blackcurrant bushes. It looks . . . different. Bushes are different from trees. There's 100 acres of blackcurrants and they're all Scottish varieties. They begin with a Ben — Ben Lomond, Ben Hope, Ben Avon, Ben Alder. The Ben Lomond come first and then you move on to the Ben Hope, and Ben Alder are the later ones, so they don't all come at once.

They used to have women come and pick the blackcurrants, pick them by hand. Then they started with the machine. We would cut all the bushes down and feed them through the machine. They would crop every other year, you see, so the blackcurrant bushes would grow up one year and we'd cut them down the next. Now we've got these straddling machines. They straddle over the bushes and have little fingers that vibrate and shake the bushes and the blackcurrants fall down on to conveyor belts. The fingers are fibreglass spindle things, so they just sort of go round like that, shaking. It's amazing, really. The blackcurrants go to the back and fall into the bins and the bins fill up. That's all for juice, you see, for Ribena. They say years ago, when they first brought these machines out down in Kent, the gypsies what used to work down there sabotaged the machines at night because they were doing them out of work.

The machines cost 40–50,000 pounds. The new one this year has gone without problems, but it needs to be maintained fairly regular before the season starts. Three weeks at the most they'll go during the season. You'll spend all that money for three weeks' work. When we're blackcurranting we work to about nine o'clock at night, weekends, just to get it in. You have to with blackcurrants, because they get ripe so quick. We'll start at half-seven and we'll work through till nine at night. We don't work Saturdays because the factory where they go is not open on a Sunday. We take a break from twelve to twelve-thirty, and a quarter of an hour at five o'clock time.

If you look under the bushes, a lot of blackcurrants lie on the floor, but we just don't worry about them. It takes so long to pick them by hand, it's so much cheaper to waste them. There's just so much that goes on the floor these days. I guess it would be frustrating if you wanted to buy a pound of blackcurrants. You see them lying there on the floor, you'd think, Why can't I go pick them up?

*He seems every bit the athlete he once was: he wears red track suit bottoms and a red sweatshirt, and his physical presence has not diminished with the years. He recently moved to a bungalow a few miles away from Akenfield. We sit in the front room as the light fades. Soon only the glow from the artificial fire illuminates the photos on the walls: pictures of him holding ripe apples, an aerial shot of the house in Akenfield where he spent most of his life. As a testament to his athletic past, he brings out an ancient football boot he's been keeping in the garage.*

I was born in Ivy Cottage, Akenfield, in 1930. Catchpole is a very old Suffolk name. There are a few Catchpoles in the grave-yard here, including my mum and dad. My grandfather worked on the farm for fifty years, my father worked on the farm for fifty years and I worked on there for fifty years, so there has been a continuation for a long while back. My grandfather helped build some of the older fruit sheds on the farm. They've stood.

At sixteen I went to my first testing with my grandfather to see how to grade colour and size. By the time I was seventeen the farmer said, 'You can be in charge of your fruit.' I took care of the fruit until the time I retired. I always felt that if you were interested in a job, then job satisfaction meant a lot. I had opportunities to go to other farms as manager or foreman. I turned them down because I was happy where I was and didn't want all the hassle. I had responsibility, which I enjoyed, and I was with nature. I'm a proper nature man and like seeing things grow up.

I was always doing sports. My wife, Jean, and I started playing tennis when we were sixteen. She was one of a family of ten. Her mother lost her husband when he was only forty-four from pneumonia, which was an after-effect of the war. He was in France and got shell-shocked and was not in a good state. So Jean was in service when she left school at fourteen. She went into a house to be the house parlour maid and she came down to my house in Akenfield on weekends. Later, we kept in touch with the chapels and joined the tennis club. In fact, it's fifty-two year ago we won a doubles tournament down at Akenfield Tennis Club. We played three matches of tennis in the morning, went off to pick gooseberries and then during the afternoon they came to us and said we had enough points to go back and play the finals. So back we went, changed into our tennis things, went out there and won the trophy.

My wife, she's only just five feet but she could serve very well. Her serve stayed low on the grass on the Akenfield courts instead of bouncing up to the height they were used to. She didn't pitch the ball very high, so her serve used to just skim over the net. That foxed a lot of the opposition.

In the tennis club we didn't play in a league; we played all friendly matches around Woodbridge, Wickham Market, Peasenhall. They were lovely village courts. There was about an acre and a quarter of ground at the vicarage in Akenfield and around 1928–30 one of the sportier vicars said he would like tennis courts. One of the farmers at Park Farm ploughed up the land. They brought the harrows in and raked this soil over and the children came out the next day with a tumble cart and picked up all the stones. At night one of the men who worked for another farmer would come down and harrow it up again. The next day the children would pick stones up. It used to slope, but they took some dirt and made it so there was a drop from one court to the other. They rounded it off so we had two courts there and that became a real lovely little tennis club. A lot of men in the village give their time voluntarily to come level the courts off with their horses. They sowed it all here by hand. There was an old man who used to cut the courts. He was what we used to call a runner for the post office, before they had bikes. When a telegram come in, he used to walk off with the telegram and come back. He cut the courts. There's always somebody cut the courts. We used to pay for the person to cut the grass. If the rate was three pound an hour what you were getting on the farm, then you paid somebody three pound an hour at night to cut the grass. That's how we done it right up.

We played on those tennis courts for decades. Then we lost them. The person who bought the vicarage three years ago was a businessman with a business in Jersey. The first year he was quite happy to let the tennis club continue. He'd got some young children who used to play as well. There was a misunderstanding once, because someone from the tennis club who didn't know went there and asked what the people were doing on the courts. Well, they were the owners. That was unfortunate. Then these people wanted more privacy. They put up the fence all the way around. They were nice enough, but they did like their privacy, you see. They decided they wanted a hard court, so what they did is they had a firm come in and put in one hard court where we used to have two grass courts. By that time we hadn't got nowhere to play. We were going to negotiate as to whether we could borrow that court. But now the house is up for sale. They're moving off. They're going back to Jersey. And the hard court just stands there now.

*

'Two members of Akenfield Tennis Club got married.' That's how the local newspaper started the piece about Jean and I. Pastor Baker married Jean's mother and father, and he married my mother and father. It's very unique that somebody would marry both sets of parents and the children. But then he was a unique man. Before being a minister he was a comedian, so he used to bring a lot of humour into the pulpit. He was one of these men with the old wax moustache – the horns – and he'd make a joke or two about that. As he curled his moustache up he would say that though they look like horns they weren't the horns of the devil, they were sticking out for the Lord. One day he come out of the manse, his house, and he got a bucket and started running up the street. He was shouting, 'Fire! Fire!' People asked where, and he said, 'In Hell, for all those who don't believe in God!' That was the sort of man he was.

He was very poorly off with the chapel. It don't get nothing from the state, you know, so we offer congregation support. He used to go to Ipswich every Tuesday and he was friendly with the butcher there. He'd go round and the butcher would always give him a joint of meat. On the Monday after the Sunday service he'd come round the village, visiting anyone sick and like that. People would give him potatoes, a few veg, a can of milk. Somebody would give him some eggs. He'd never ask for anything but he was given.

I served forty-eight years being a deacon. It's a responsible position to have. When you was in the church the pastor would be keeping a watchful eye on your character, not just on your Sunday attendance, and also on your wife to see if you were together in things, to be able to take the post as a deacon. You had to be an example to others, to help to form character, to see after the elderly and the children who need teaching. I carried on till I was seventy and I felt then I should retire – not resign, retire. The church were very good when I retired. They give me a nice garden seat to sit on. I've got it out the back.

We used to be called 'strict Baptists', which was a name nobody really liked. Why they said 'strict' is because we believed in a closed communion table. But the 'strict' put people off rather than encouraging them. We had about twenty-eight or thirty members. The lowest we dropped down to was eighteen; we are now up to twenty-one. The eighteen was mainly because the whole problem with Akenfield is lack of housing. Some go to university and don't come back. Other ones, if they want to get away they get to Ipswich or somewhere like that. When they marry there are no houses so they've got to get away. At the other end of the scale, my mum and my grandma are all dying off. But last year we had one family move in from somewhere up in London. They've got a family of four girls, and two of the girls were converted and asked to be baptized, so that took our numbers up.

When we have a baptismal service, it's done by full immersion. The baptistry now is in the middle of the chapel. It's covered up with boards and we've got an organ on top. We take that off and when we have a baptismal service we let it be known the church is having it and the chapel is virtually full. People will come and sit in the gallery, people perhaps who have nothing to do with religion at all. If we give a baptism they like to come and see what we're doing. Beneath the boards there's about four steps you go down. The water comes about halfway up. We have a service first, the person getting baptized changes into white clothes and then they go down into the water. I was baptized in my cricket kit, because I used to play cricket for Dallinghoo. My wife had a tennis outfit and was baptized in that; they used to put little lead weights in the pleat of the skirt to keep it from coming up in the water. Come to think of it, Jean's was probably the same tennis uniform she was wearing when we won the doubles tournament at Akenfield Tennis Club.

*

There used to be social evenings in villages like Akenfield. Now the most people get together is when we have the flower show, which has kept on. It must have been going well over fifty years now. There used to always be the church fête, a big occasion in June. Well, now they haven't got a vicar in the village. The lady vicar they've got now has to see over five different churches and there hasn't been a fête for four, five year now. Them occasions have disappeared, sadly. They were occasions when the village people mingled together. In the summertime, in the orchard where I worked, you'd get a gang of about a dozen, fifteen women. They were all together and there was a sort of community spirit. Now the machines have come on and where we used to have 100 people picking the blackcurrants, now two machines do the lot. Gooseberries are gone too. The children used to come along and pick no end of gooseberries.

We used to have the old Suffolk horses. We used to have herds of cows, pigs. They're all gone now. On the way to Akenfield now there's a pig farm there, but they're all shut up in the buildings. You can go right by in the car and nobody would even know it's a pig farm there.

And the way people look has changed. Workers' hands have changed no end. The old boys – we used to call them that when we went on the farm – their hands were big rough, hoary hands, horny hands. They'd be using them in the harvest time with the pitchfork, grappling the stave of a fork about an inch and a quarter diameter. During the wintertime they'd be having a digging fork and they done a lot of hedging and cleaned the ditches out. I know they had gloves on, but their hands were great big wide hands with tough old skin. I mean, my hands are worker's hands. I even lost a finger when I was working on the soil bench at the back of a combine. Their hands now are completely different.

The clothes are so much different too. When I first went to work I was pleased as anything to have a pair of boots like the old boys had. They were great big boots and they were all studs and hobs, as we used to call them. You know, all metal. Gracious me, nowadays you wouldn't be able to lift them off the floor, hardly. Then they'd have buskins to keep the dirt and that out. Wellies weren't very much used in them days. That was always the thing – have a good old pair of them hobnailed boots and have these old buskins around here to keep you dry, keep your mud from your trousers. In the wintertime you'd be digging in the ditch and the water would be running away and you'd get splashed all up with water and mud.

Even when I started working the machines it affected my hands. When you got on the back of the machine, the blackcurrants were constantly coming at you all the while, you see. You had a tray that held twenty-eight pound and as they come through you had to keep them moving. Your hands were in blackcurrant juice nearly all the time and blackcurrants are not the pleasantest thing; the juice is rather sticky and sweet. Thankfully I wasn't a smoker, but if someone wanted a fag they'd roll it and get blackcurrant juice all over the cigarette. Even if you wanted a sweet, you'd get juice all over. We'd just have an ordinary bucket with water because we were in the open field, a thirty-acre field, and you'd have an old piece of rag there and wash your hands as best you could and get your tea. Now, thankfully, the blackcurrant machines have got these boxes on the back where the currants just go. Somebody's still got to stand there; if a leaf or two go in, you pick them out.

The blackcurrants was the worst time on the farm because we used to start at seven in the morning and we kept at it till half-past eight at night. You was out there on the back of the machine. You had the heat of the machine, the heat of the day, the drum of the machine, the dust coming off the bushes. That was terrible working, that was. That went on for three weeks and that was the three weeks I detested most on the farm. That was about the only three weeks on the farm when I was tied down to a machine, because the rest of the while I was nearly my own boss. I would do my own fertilizing and take care of the women. But when it got to a machine I was tied to that from half-past seven to half-past eight. That wasn't me at all.

Machinery has advanced tremendously well. I said they'd never get a machine to do the blackcurrants. They were so soft, they'd squash when we used to pick 'em. We had the first machine come there and that made a terrible job of it. I said, 'There, what did I say?' Next year the machines were a little bit better. Now they've got a machine that do it better than the women. I was proved wrong after all my years' experience on the farm. The machines are doing a better job than what the hand-pickers do.

When I was on the farm, for forty years they were all just open tractors. You sit there in all the elements. We used to have a sack or a rug over our knees to keep warm, to keep the wind out as you were going along. Now they got the cabs there, power-steering, you can sit in there and steer away. You got a radio in there. I'm pleased for the boys what are out there now, but they can sit in there like it was an armchair. The seats are sprung, whereby we used to have a solid little thing with your bones shaking about all day long.

I like the view from the Ipswich road, the 1078. Around you are the hawthorns, and the sloes and blackberries. You'd think, Oh, that's beautiful. If you stand up there you can see in the distance the church and the vicarage and then look right across the valley to the fruit trees, which are all dead in line. Then you can see a white cottage up there. That's where I used to live. I've still got a good heart for Akenfield, where I've been living all my life. I ain't got no regrets in moving; I'm quite happy here. But as I come by that way, I look across there and the memories are coming back. I think, Right, I spent my life going to the village school. I was brought up there. I went there when I was about three and a half to start school, playing about. And then my life was centred around the village. I can see the field where I worked. And I must say there's pride in all them trees, because they're always planted on a square. Whichever way you looked, there were rows. We used to plant them eighteen feet squared and if you looked this way, that way, corner ways, they all come in dead straight.

My wife says they could come in here and take the clock and I wouldn't notice it was gone, but if they took a flower out of the garden I'd miss it. Give me a television set or a Hoover and I know nothing about it at all, but give me a rake and a fork and I'm an expert.

## ARTHUR PECK
### FORMER ORCHARD FOREMAN, 89

*In the sheltered accommodation where he lives, there is a hiss of fluorescence and the wheelchair lift makes a regular journey from the hall to the first floor. He has a shock of white hair. 'Several people have told me I've got a lovely head of hair,' he says, touching it in slight disbelief that it's still there. 'I don't deny it. My uncle on my mother's side was ninety-nine and he'd still got hair and that.' He settles himself into a comfortable chair. He doesn't have the energy to do much, he says, but he still drives to Akenfield to attend services at the Baptist chapel, where he sits stiffly in his shirt and tie and afterwards is surrounded by people, who slowly shake his hand and say, 'Good to see you, Arthur.' The loud ticking of his clock echoes in the room.*

When I went to the bank two or three years ago, I had to fill in some papers. The lady at the bank asked me my full name and I said, 'Arthur Ephraim Peck.'

She said, 'Never heard of it.' Ephraim, she meant.

I said, 'I've got an uncle with that name and a grandfather with that name.'

And when she filled the form in, she'd spelt it 'Ephrime'. I suppose it's an old Bible name really.

I was born in 1915 at Hoo. We moved to Akenfield when I was three years old. My father used to work on the farm. I was only six when my father died, and I can't honestly say how he died, but they say it was bronchitis. After my father died my mother was getting ten shillings a week pension, five shillings from me and three shillings from my sister. So we was getting eighteen shillings a week to live on and pay the rent and everything. We were hard up.

When I was eight, the farmer's wife said, 'If you'd like to come down and work on a Saturday morning, you can have a little job getting the sticks and wood in,' so I used to walk down there nearly two mile and get the sticks in. I was kitchen boy, if you like to call me. I got eightpence – eight old pennies – on a Saturday morning. I'd take it home to my mother. Somebody tried to persuade my mother to put us into a Dr Barnardo's home, but my mother said no. While she could scrape anything together she wouldn't want to part with her children. So what she done at that time was this: there used to be several Dr Barnardo children in the village, from London or somewhere thereabouts. So my mother put in for it and she got three children. So from what money she got off them and her pension, we just managed all right.

I worked at the big house. I chopped sticks to light the fire with. I carted them into the big shed, filled the baskets up and swept the parlours. That's what I done till I left school. When I left school I just done farmwork. You couldn't leave till you was fourteen. When they broke up for holidays in July or August, my birthday came a fortnight before. So I didn't have to go back to school.

I did what jobs needed to be done. I was on a fruit farm doing apple picking. Otherwise I used to work with the horses. We'd got seven horses on our farm, three horsemen. When the three of them used to go plough, they had two horses each, and that left one horse to do odd jobs. Sometimes two of the horsemen would do the drilling and us youngsters would do the harrowing with a pair of horses. I'd walk miles harrowing the land. My feet used to get so sore. When we first were doing it in the spring-time, I was picked to lead a horse. They used to have a horse with a set of hoes that were the width of a drill. They were hoes set so they'd go in between each row of corn. That's how they kept the fields fairly clean. It used to stop the rubbish from coming up.

Bernard Catchpole's grandfather used to be in the fruit sheds. Eventually he gave up and the boss asked me to take over the fruit. So I was in charge of the women and the blackcurrant picking. We had over eighty women and children. They used to come at eight o'clock in the morning and work till eight or nine o'clock. The children used to come straight here from school instead of going home for tea, so they could earn a little money. They'd say, 'Can I have a number, Mr Peck?' If you had a number, you see, you could earn money. If they were with their mother, it went on the mother's number. Would they ever work hard! I seen the women sit underneath a tree in the shade, sweat would be running off them. They'd have about an hour and then they'd come right back again.

When I first went to that farm, we had a horse and trolley to take the fruit up the cartways. I went to see the farm at harvest time and travelled up and down the cartways with Bernard's father. If there was a wind and it blew some apples down, we had to walk ahead of the cart and push them apples out of the way with our feet so they didn't get squashed. Every now and again, we picked them up and took them to a wholesaler in Ipswich, who sold them to several shops. The chap who drove the lorry, he'd come back and say they wanted another load of them dropped apples. There's one sort of pear – Emile d'Heyst – that was a big pear. We'd walk round the pear trees with little bags, put those pears in and tie the tops. You pulled them up, you see, over the pear and just loosely tied them to the tree, so if they dropped they couldn't drop on to the ground. The bags were thin – not exactly paper, but close. That was the value of those pears.

Pay used to vary. The farmer set the price more or less for the average worker: what you'd be getting if you were doing so much per hour. Some weren't so quick, so they had a real job earning money. Other ones earned double. The quicker ones used to do quite well. There were the quick and the clean. When you'd look in the buckets of some, there used to be more leaves than there was fruit. I'd say to them, 'You'd better pick the leaves out before you go back.' When you look in the baskets of others, all fruit.

The quickest and cleanest pickers were my wife's family. There were three of them girls. Some people used to come and buy blackcurrants right from the farm, so I always used to have someone standing by to pick. I needed someone who could pick clean and not many leaves. That family were the quickest and cleanest pickers we'd got; they were the ones you could rely on. They knew you just had to snap the blackcurrants. You got to be sure. When you're picking you've got next year's bud on there as well. If you pick them off, then you don't have a crop for next year. Clean picking was a true skill.

My wife, Winnie – actually it's Nora, but she always went as Winnie; even on her gravestone, it says Nora but it also has Winnie – after we got married and after the children got big enough to go to school, she used to walk down to work on the farm. You couldn't keep her off it. I wouldn't be there more than half an hour and she'd come down the road. I'd say, 'What you doing here, Winnie?' She'd say, 'I got nothing else to do. I thought I'd come.' And she'd be one of the last ones to go. She knew how to pick.

We used to have wild oats out in the corn. We had it bad on our farm – as they did on the other farms – and our boss used to say to the women, 'Go pull them wild oats.' They'd have to carry the oats out in bags and put them on the headland. There was one woman, she could sing, she could. We were pulling wild oats one day. I was just over the field. She got on to singing – she was a Cockney, although she married my wife's brother. He picked her up during the war. When she used to sing aloud sometimes there'd be a shouting from across where they were building the bungalows. The men working there could hear her. 'Give us another one, dear!' they'd yell.

I helped them plant almost every tree that's on the farm now. In my time they planted trees. The first year I worked there they planted about ten acres of plums. And about two years after that, me and another chap planted another fifteen acres. In that time of day they had to be dead straight down the row. If they were out of hand, we would have to pull them all up and replant them so they were dead straight.

My son Malcolm started at the orchard when he was fifteen. He picked it up off us, I suppose. When he was a little boy, he loved to be out in the garden. He'd hoe in between my onions just as well as we would. That grew on him.

When I was retiring, the boss said to me, 'You retire in August, don't you, Arthur?'

I said, 'Yes.'

'Have you got anybody you can recommend to take your place?'

I said, 'No.'

'You think about it,' he said. He left it about a fortnight and came back and said, 'Have you thought about anybody?'

I said, 'I only know two who I can recommend,' and I told him.

'I haven't heard of them two,' he said. 'Why don't we talk about Malcolm?'

Malcolm! I never even dreamt it. I knew he was as good as

them but it never even entered my head. He was young, you see. 'He'd be all right,' I said, 'but I don't know whether he'd take it. The responsibility.'

He said, 'You ask him.'

I sat down with Malcolm and he gave it a thought. He said, 'Yes, I don't mind.' And that's how he became foreman.

I don't suppose I would have told Malcolm to do something else. But I never dreamt things would change. There were twenty-five of us when I went down to the orchard to work. When I gave up and Malcolm took over, there was fifteen men left. Now there's three of them.

For years after Malcolm took over everything was in full swing. Army men were coming and buying up land and planting ten or twenty acres. There were young trees. All our fruit went to cold storage. There used to be a canning factory down in Woodbridge. We used to send over ten tonnes of plums for them to can from our place. It weren't just apples.

I suppose it all gradually changed and we didn't take notice of it. The other week I sat here thinking about the fruit on the farm and so I wrote down all the names I could. On one side, all the plums we used to grow and on the other all the apples I can remember that used to be on the farm.* There's over thirty different apples we grew on that farm. Mind you, don't try and read the spelling, 'cause I'm a very poor speller.

Victoria plums sold better than any. I don't know why. More flavour, I suppose. They used them for jam and everything. It's surprising how many plums are there what are named after birds. There's a mallard, curlew, swan, bittern, heron – all named after birds. They're nonexistent now. I don't know nobody what's got a plum orchard. The farm where we are, they've only got three or four different sorts of plums. And half them get dropped and never get sold.

* See the appendix.

I think the time's a-coming when there won't be any fruit there. All they're doing now is planting blackcurrants. When we first started we used to pick them by hand, then it got so they used machines. One of the women said to the farmer one day, 'Time is coming when you won't want us.'

'Yes, we will,' he said. 'We shall always have hand-picking for you together.'

But the time did come when they didn't want the women. We used to irrigate the orchard and put on frost protection. Now they've done away with it.

I'll always remember our old governor, one of them, he used to say, 'Don't put your eggs all in one basket.'

They used to grow clover. He grew two fields, but he'd never let you put one in until he saw the other one coming up. Now that's all they're doing – putting everything in blackcurrants. Just one set of bad frosts . . . and that's gone.

I go back to the orchard every other Wednesday. I generally go up to the orchard and I pick some fruit. They told me when I retired, 'If ever you want anything, Arthur, you just help yourself.' So I go up there and get some when I want some. During the winter perhaps I'll ride through the orchard like a poor old farmer, wondering what's happened. I used to go walking through that orchard when I was eight year old and still go walking through, and that's eighty-one year ago. I can't help it. I say that I don't like to see it, but there's nothing I can do about it. I'm happy down there.

There won't be another foreman. There'll be nobody there to be foreman over! I mean, all these farms – in Wickham Market, they had a big orchard and pulled all their apple trees out, turned it all into arable land. Now they've sold all the land, kept the house and the chap what was foreman there, they kept him on in the gardens for about a year, and then he was old enough to retire. That's how things go.

Funny thing, I hate the taste of blackcurrants. And blackcurrant jam, I wouldn't eat it. My mother, when we were small, she used to make what you call blackcurrant drink. She would put a spoonful or two spoonfuls of blackcurrant jam into a cup and boil the water and used to give it to us for colds. It used to wear off on our hands. Sometimes when the women used to come in the next morning you wouldn't know their hands were the same as when they went in the night before. Now gooseberries, I liked gooseberries, I could eat them. I had one of them in my mouth . . . I'd be sucking on one of those nearly all day.

And I don't eat any apples uncooked. Whatever apples I eat, I stew; I don't care if they're eaters or cookers. I can't eat apples and I don't like blackcurrants. It don't sound right, do it?

*Incomers*

KEITH GIPP
RETIREE, 57

*He and his wife, Jill, retired to Akenfield and live in the old schoolhouse. All the neighbours say how much better it looks now that they have renovated it. The bricks that were spoiled from frost have been replaced; new windows have been added. His father was a master builder. 'He would have loved to have worked on this place if he were still around. He'd still be clinging to the brickwork.' He is happy to have got out of the workforce before age sixty. When you're retired, he says, the weeks just seem to disappear. They keep a boat moored in Woodbridge and spend time walking the fields. Once a week he works at the local airfield, taking care of odd jobs and repairs.*

I was born in London, in Wandsworth. I met my wife, Jill, thirty-one and a half years ago and we settled in Surrey. I met Jill in a bank in Surbiton, a Barclays. I went in to install a telephone and I made it take five hours. I said to the senior technician, 'I've seen this girl – give me more time.' It ended up being a day and a half of fault time.

We moved here because we'd had enough of the rat race. To get two miles in Surrey it took twenty minutes. We didn't like the graffiti, the manners of the kids. It used to be lovely. But the traffic got worse and the whole idea was rush, rush, rush. We had to leave Surrey. The young – I say the young, I mean twelve upwards – they didn't seem to have any respect. Our house was semi-detached and the kids next door could overlook us. There were two boys and they fired a hand airgun at our cat. I saw it happen. I know they lost their father at a young age. Their mother was out. The boyfriend was out. I lost my temper, as you would. I went over. They had locked themselves in the loo. The language coming out of that loo! I broke in, kicked the door in and chased them up the stairs. You would not have believed the things they were saying.

We had a row of conifers. The family next door cut five of them down and threw them over the side of the fence. See, I've always brought children up to be respectful. This was the final straw.

When we moved up here we had criteria: we wanted to have access to a main town but we wanted to be rural. This place was well within our price range. We knocked on the front door and we were welcomed in by the owner. We felt it immediately. We gave each other a nod. We stood in the front door, looked back at each other and then said, 'Yes, we'll have it.' The owner was a little bemused, since we had only just stepped in the door. But it was as if we were home. It felt right. It was the luxury of looking out of the windows of the house and not seeing anyone. It was wheat out there. The other field was fallow. We were worried that they might build a housing estate or something, not knowing you can't build on rural land. As we left we said, 'We'll ring the estate agent.' We got in the car and rang him on the mobile.

When we moved in, the village newsletter said, 'We wish to welcome Keith and Jill to the village.' You wouldn't get a hello in Surrey. We went to the first village meeting. Don Ewings, who was running the meeting, had a big pile of paperwork near him. He said, 'I want to nominate someone to be chairman.' No one put their hand up. Don looked at me. 'Would you become chairman?' he said. I had only been in the village five minutes!

We lost two cats when we came out here. They weren't country cats, they were urban cats. I don't think they were used to the country life. One of our neighbours just said one day, 'Bring a blanket. Your cat's in the road.' Your entire attitude towards animals changes when you become a rural person. In Surrey we had a fox and cubs that came and visited our house. We'd feed them dog biscuits and chicken bones. Our dogs got used to them. They'd sit and wait for the food. Now here, when you see a fox, you try and get a gun before it's run off.

We used to rescue mice. Now we just kill them. When we came up, we put a lot of our stuff in the garage. We came in July and just slung it out in the garage. All my fishing gear, my nets and even the umbrellas have been ruined by mice. Now we know to put our food in tins. We know it's survival of the fittest.

If you see a rabbit in Surrey – lovely. They're not so nice out here. Rural people have a harder attitude. You hear them out there in the fields shooting pigeons, as many as they can get their hands on. You see these rabbits with myxomatosis and at the beginning you think, Poor thing, should we take it to the vet's? You eventually realize it's better to put it out of its misery. This poor blind thing that can hardly get across the road. I now get hold of its back legs and break its neck on a tree. I wouldn't have dreamt of doing that in Surrey.

If you think the country will be quiet, you'll be surprised. There's the rookery nearby. There are 100 rooks up there. The noise is incredible – a continuous squawking, like a crescendo going up and up. In the spring they have their babies and you can't even hear yourself think. They all go into the air if they're disturbed and squawk even more.

You learn about animals. I was over at the local airfield, where I was doing some restoration work. This was when the corn was high. I heard this noise and thought, What is that? A two-day-old baby duck came running out. From the local hatcheries you can only hear the sound of the occasional quack. Here was an escaped duck. It came over and sat on my hand. Oh dear, I thought. I phoned Jill and told her I'd just found a baby duck. Soft as I am, we kept it and got a heat lamp for it. Now, I'd put money on the fact that this duck thinks he's actually a dog. The duck goes wherever the dogs go. The duck even regularly attacks one of the dogs, and the dog in turn gets the duck's head in his mouth and carries him around by his neck. The duck lives in the garage at night, with a glass door so he can look out. Everyone knows our duck. Even the postman. He'll stop and not just throw the letters in the postbox. 'Can I see your duck who thinks he's a dog?' he'll say. In Surrey I couldn't even tell you what the postman looked like.

A few weeks ago I could hear guns going off in the field in the daytime, which was quite unusual. We've got a bedroom with both windows facing the field. I looked out and there was a combine going up and down the field. There was a young man, twenty-five or twenty-six, running along with a carbine, hitting rabbits as they were coming out. I don't think he missed one rabbit in about half an hour. He wrung their necks. It was all professionally done. The whole time they were harvesting the field. I went out there and told him I wished I could shoot like that. 'I'm in the army,' he said, 'on long-term leave.' He asked me if I wanted a couple of rabbits. He said, 'Leave it with me.' Later there were six rabbits laid out at my front door, and they weren't small either. They were in good health. We've had to learn to cut the feet off, take the head off, the skin. I did all the gutting; Jill skinned. As long as the guts are out she's fine with it.

I've learned a lot about country ways. In summer, in the fields, the skylarks nest in the ground. They sing so beautifully. What I've found is that when they go to ground, when they land, they land a few feet away from the nest and walk back, so you don't know where the nest is. There are so many little things to be learned. The maize in the fields – I stupidly thought it was sweetcorn at first.

I enjoy the country. I enjoy living here. You know a little when you arrive and the rest comes as you progress. It smells different. We keep the windows open at night. There were one or two stars we used to see in Surrey. We see them all here. We try to appreciate it. There are those who move out here and say, 'Oh, we need street lights.' Not us. We try to blend in. Certain people are more afraid of townies like us coming here and changing them into townies. No, no, we're the opposite. We want to be like the country people.

*She was born in Kent and from an early age was involved in the church. 'It's part of my background,' she says. She now attends a 'fairly evangelical' Church of England a few miles from Akenfield that is focused on youth – a creche for infants like her son Jamie and a class called Scramblers for three–five year olds, like her daughter Hannah. She lives in a converted farm worker's cottage with her husband, Rick. When they first moved in, the police showed up at the door because a neighbour saw a light. There is a sort of watchful eye, she says, but it is appreciated. This afternoon Rick helps Hannah with her arts and crafts while Jamie cheerfully gums a cookie. Before the children, Julie worked as a teacher. Julie gave birth to Jamie in this front room. She was in bed by eleven o'clock that evening. 'I still didn't sleep, mind you. He slept. It's a buzz, really. I just lay there with all the adrenalin, thinking "He is breathing, isn't he? He is breathing".'*

Neither Rick nor I are rural people by nature but when we saw this property everything just, you know . . . fitted. We could get to work in the middle of Ipswich in twenty minutes but we were also near to Rick's parents, who live in a village. We needed to find a house with off-road parking. We needed space, because Rick rebuilds motorbikes.

I used to imagine living here and remember thinking, Goodness me, we really will be in the middle of nowhere. I imagined there would be no street lights. I imagined this darkness, complete dark, so that you can see the sky. I was a little bit scared thinking about it. Instead we get the glow from the warehouse. There's a hum from over there.

Our place had been redeveloped from a farm worker's cottage already. It was still old-fashionedy but completely done up. It had a bit of character, cosiness. We were a few years away from having kids but there was enough space for the beginnings of a family. We knew there was potential.

Here you always have to travel in the car. Ideally we would like to have places we could walk to and meet up with people – more of a community feel. I would have imagined there would be more of that in the countryside: walking around the village, bumping into people you know and knowing one another in a supportive way. That would be in the back of my mind as to what it should be like to live in a village. But we don't actually have that here.

The local characters are quite reserved. It is quite hard to get to know some. They're not being rude in any way, just careful. That said, we know all the people and I know I could ask anyone for help if I needed it. But it's not easy to meet up, it's not a natural meeting place. We don't walk anywhere, so we don't bump into anybody. I hadn't thought that through at the time of moving here. There are people in the village you always wave to, but because you don't naturally bump into people it's hard to build a proper relationship with them. We've got this fast road, this dangerous road, with big lorries going through what is really just a little hamlet.

I am chair of the Akenfield Under Fives, but it's by default really. I think there's about twenty-two in the group, and then all of their children, often one, two or three each. We buy toys and coffee because we like to have proper coffee. There are two groups. There's a local group who have been connected to this part of the world for a long time but mainly it's people who have moved up here because their husbands work at BT or another company. I don't think we're cliquey, so I don't mean it like that. It's just there are people . . . I don't really know how to say it without seeming awful. Just different classes, if you like, different backgrounds. There are the village folk, and people who have come in and have had perhaps a wider experience. There are people who have said to me they've never travelled out of Suffolk because there was no motorway.

Most of the mothers are working mums who are having a break at the moment. They're quite dynamic women – they work in mental health, there are various PAs, loads of accountants. I think we shy away from too rural a look. We want to be quite aware of what's going on. Normally we talk about children and illnesses and food and trying to cope with the organization of the day. We complain about the doctors. All the usual stuff. But I suppose some of us talk about how to get people involved, raising money, the theatre, what we've seen, what we're into. We go to the Wolsey, the main theatre in Ipswich, which has just had a brilliant production on of a Sondheim musical. We have make-up evenings to try on moisturizers and things.

All of us talk about going back to work and how we might do it – how much money you can earn against child care, whether it's worth going back to work just to keep your career going or just to get away for a while. There are ways of telling people it's OK to stay at home for a while or for as long as you want. At my book group, one girl said, 'I'm actually really enjoying this time, making jam and doing all those housey things.' She was quite proud to admit that. And I think there is a choice for some of us who don't have to work. We can make do for a while. It's trying to make the most of this time.

*

As a young mother, you need a little bit of time away from the children. Every week I'd like to have two hours without them, just to go into Woodbridge or even into Ipswich would be nice. Just to wander around and browse. I don't do any browsing any more. Catalogue shopping and Internet shopping are a big thing now. We use Tesco Direct every few weeks. We get everything from them, all the vegetables and meat and groceries and the dried foods as well. The nappies and stuff. I don't get newspapers from them. Every two or three weeks I'll do a big order and then I'll pop to Wickham Market to get the bits. I thought when we set it up that I'd be going to all the local farm shops and getting the lovely fresh food and then just getting all the toilet rolls and cereals from Tesco's. That was the original plan. But it's just worked out this way. It's easier. If these two are asleep I can't leave them in the car and go shopping. I have to wake them up to go into the shops and pay to park the car.

I do hate it. I hate Tesco's having a monopoly. I always say I'm determined, once our son Jamie's going to nursery school and I have that freedom, to go via a farm shop on the way home. There's one not too far that sells fruit and vegetables, cheese, homemade cakes, meat. Farm produce. I'd like to . . . But again it always involves journeys by car.

It seems strange saying this when you live in the countryside, but if I could easily access farm-shop produce I would. It does come down to ease. We got our bread on Thursday from the little shop attached to the garage in Akenfield. That was the beginning of us trying to buy local things. And then we stopped. I do want to support the local farmers. I think it's because Rick and I have only just come out of surviving Jamie's early years. I never knew it was so hard. You have all these ideas of being greener and more environmentally aware and it all goes to pot for a couple of years. But the aim is definitely to work back.

Tesco's makes it so easy. You just go through the list and tick off what you want. Once you've set up the system you have your favourites in and you can click on how many of everything you want. You can add on extra items, or tidy up your list and get rid of baby items you don't need any more. It's great.

Anything else means using a car. It really annoys me when I hear the government talking about car owners as if we are really naughty. The thing is, we have to rely on a car here. There are no other choices. Everything has been taken away. There aren't local shops. They haven't been taken away by the government, but it's the government that has enabled the big superstores to develop, isn't it? They've encouraged it. So therefore there aren't the options. We will always have to travel by car. There's got to be changes but it shouldn't really be our fault. It's not because we've done something wrong that we have this. We just have to live with the situation as it is now, really.

In the meantime, you have to be so organized. Get loads of something and always have spares. Two packs of Weetabix as opposed to one. When one's finishing I can move straight into the next one.

## PATRICK BISHOPP
### ENTREPRENEUR, 32

❧

*He has a knack for creating a warm, jovial atmosphere. His first job was at Harrods selling Geo F. Trumper shaving products. He shaved before the interview, 'though I had to be careful – I get quite bad rashes.' He reads books by successful British businessmen – Dyson and Branson – and keeps in shape with a good four-mile run which takes him past Akenfield Hall. The inside of his house features an original mullioned window, as well as some exposed beams which have held the house up for centuries. Outside the gleaming, renovated kitchen there are side table photographs of his wife, Sarah, and their two sons. 'She is a Yorkshire lass turned London girl,' he says with a smile. 'And I dragged her kicking and screaming to flat old Suffolk.'*

I moved to Suffolk when I was eleven, from the Midlands. Went to university, spent six years in London, met my wife, Sarah, had my first child and knew straight away when we had that child that I would leave London. I think Suffolk's one of those counties people tend to come back to. It's a bit of a community. And there are the pluses – it's an hour from London, we're by the coast, it's very beautiful. It's a very friendly place. Even though I only came here when I was eleven, Suffolk is the place I'm from.

When I was in London it was a great time to be in the Internet and I've been in the Internet ever since. Now this is my first time out of it and I'm actually really glad to be out of it. When we came here we looked at setting up an Internet advertising site for small businesses in Suffolk who couldn't afford a big fancy website. My aim was to bring all these companies together, charge them 1,000 pounds a year. They would get a little website and they would advertise my own website as a sort of directory of local Suffolk companies. It became obvious after four or five months of researching that Suffolk just wasn't really ready. The Internet was at the stage where everyone was wary and wasn't really seeing where it was going or how it worked. They weren't willing to stick 1,000 pounds of their marketing budget in.

After six months my wife and I decided we weren't really willing to invest any more of our time and money into it. It wasn't a small amount, so we hedged our bets and said, 'Fine, it's not something we're going to follow up. It will be on the back burner.' We could always get all the files out and start it up again. It got to the stage where there were five people working there, so it was a proper business – but we never launched it.

That left us in a situation where I thought, What do I do next? Do I retrain? However lovely Suffolk is, the biggest flaw about Suffolk is jobs. There's just hardly any well-paid jobs in Suffolk. It's at the end of the road. You only come to Suffolk because you're going there. I was really struggling. I joined lots of recruitment companies. Not one phone call. I could have been over-qualified. I've always worked for small companies. My roles have always been making sales. I started off in brushes and razors, and then moved into the Internet, so I've got a varied CV. But I think a lot of companies just didn't think out of the box. It got me thinking, Are we just living a dream in being here? It's lovely, but in reality we have to support a family. I thought, Am I just looking in the wrong place?

We did it the wrong way round. We should have found a career before moving instead of just moving and thinking, Right, we're here now, what next? If we did the whole thing again it would be a career move, a job move, not a lifestyle move. But we wanted to make this our family home. It used to be a classic farm but over the years it's turned, as most farmhouses have, into an unclassic farm. We plan to be here for the rest of our lives.

When we moved here, we'd meet people and they'd say, 'Oh, you're the Internet guy from London.' They knew everything about me already, which is very much village life. I think we have been accepted, but we've only met a very small part of the village, even as a small community. I think it'll change over time. We've only been here two and a half years.

I think people are very intrigued by us. We are a young couple; I worked in the Internet. I'm seen walking my dog during the day, when most men are out at work, so I get a lot of comments like, 'Is it your day off? Working from home today?' A lot of people trying to get an answer without asking direct questions, like, 'What are you doing walking your dog during the day? Why aren't you earning money?' But I'm not an Internet millionaire.

I'm not a religious man. But my wife Sarah goes every now and then to church with our son Angus. In Akenfield you've got the Baptists and you've got the Church of England, and there's a divide between them. The Baptist minister came round here when we first moved in and he knocked on our door, as any nice church vicar would, and he said 'welcome to the village'. He said, 'Will we be seeing you?' I told him that Angus had just been christened and he's going to be going to the other church. And he said, 'Oh, that's really bad. We don't do that in our church. We wait till they're old enough and make our own decisions.' And then my wife told him he shouldn't try to persuade me, that I'm an atheist. He looked at me and said, 'Well, you're going to die in eternal hell,' or something like that. If we hadn't just moved in I would have kicked him out of the driveway. But I just told him that I wasn't interested. The other vicar is great – she christened Jacoby.

There are people here who get involved in the village and people who would never think about helping out. I kind of see myself in the middle: I'm not the kind of person who's going to spend lots of time organizing village fêtes and so on, but when someone asks me to help out I'm happy to do it. Like today, for example, I got a call saying, 'Would you mind being a horse?' They're looking at doing a human horse race, it turns out. I don't know how it works but I said fine. If they had said they needed me to organize the race, then I would have said no. So I'm part of the village, very much so, but I'm not a footsoldier. My family comes first before anything. That may sound selfish, but I think that's what community is all about: making sure families work and can mix together.

We want to be part of the village but there's so much life outside the village now. And there's no shop here, and there's no post office. The village hasn't got that central meeting point that other villages have. It's also in prime commuting territory. I don't see the point of living in a place like this and never seeing it.

One of the saddest things about this village – and I think it really stops the village from being as close as it could be – is that we haven't had a good village pub for a long time. When I was sixteen, seventeen, eighteen, my parents used to eat in the local pub here two or three times a week. It was a lovely village pub, with a really good landlord, who did really good food. It looked like a country pub, felt like a country pub. It was popular. He left. Hasn't been the same since. The last owner went for a wine-bar look, which to me is like an IKEA look. It didn't have a village atmosphere, that was the problem. It just wasn't a lovely village pub you felt you could go in and sit down and have a few drinks and chat to the locals. If Akenfield had that kind of pub it would be a much better village and a much closer village as well.

And it's no cheaper living out here than it is living in London. That's a myth. It is, I'm sorry. I'll dispute the food is slightly cheaper. Tesco anywhere is going to be the same price. Local food is probably the same. Pub food: Suffolk for some reason has become a real gourmet-pub place. You're very hard pressed now to find really good pub grub that isn't London prices. What you're saving on other things you'll spend on petrol. We've got two cars and we probably do a tank a car each week. That's eighty quid a week!

After my last idea failed, I made the very conscious decision that I didn't want to be a salesman any more. I don't think I'm hard enough to be a salesman. I think I'm too honest. It got to the stage where I really didn't want to spend my day phoning companies and trying to sell things and 90 per cent of the time being told there's no one here. I've been doing it all my life now. My father did sales. He invented those perfume samplers you get in magazines, the ones where you peel off a plastic film. He invented that. He got a patent on that and sold it to an American company. There's quite a few different ones. People always get it confused with the long strips. It's not that one. It's the one where literally you peel off a little film. The patent is the perfume in the ink. He's a pure salesman, through and through. I obviously didn't get the genes.

So I started thinking, What do I really want to do? What's my passion? It's food. I love cooking. I love sourcing food and buying food. I'm a real foodie. Sarah was saying I should do something with food, and I came across the idea that it's really hard to source local produce.

I'm a real Tesco-ite. If we need to do a shop we go to Tesco's because it's on the way to Angus's school. It's on the way to everything. If you ever try to go shopping with two children, you can't pull up to a small farm shop and drag the children out and to another place.

I looked at the whole local-produce thing. My initial idea was to wholesale local produce to pubs, restaurants and shops and get them to start buying locally sourced produce instead of going to the big wholesalers and just buying the cheapest stuff they could find. While I was researching I spoke to a couple of suppliers and they asked, 'Why don't you sell it directly to the consumer?' So I looked into that angle. To have a localized Tesco Direct.

Let's say you wanted to buy some really good local sausages, some local bacon, good local fruit and veg, a couple of pork pies and some chutneys. At the moment to buy locally you'd probably have to go to three or four different places. What I'm offering is really good local food: come to me and, instead of having to drive to all these places to pick it up, I'll come to you. If I can bring that convenience and a similar service but have local produce, then there's no reason why people won't buy it. They'll still have to go to the shops. I won't be selling loo rolls or washing-up liquid.

This isn't an Internet company. I'm just using the Internet as a tool for ordering. So people will be able to order by telephone, they can email me, fax me, stick a stamp on an envelope. It's right across the board, because I think it's all about choice. Some people like to use the Internet, some people like to pick up the phone. My dad, for example, he just wants to send a fax over.

I don't have a van yet. I will. I've got to source a good second-hand van. Locally. But in ten years' time I'd like to think there will be about twenty vans, every day doing every part of East Anglia – picking up and dropping off food.

Eventually maybe other counties would have a look at it. The worst outcome is that no one orders from it. But I'm going to stick with it. Even if it means doing night shifts at Tesco's to make it work.

*The Only One in the Village*

## REV. BETTY MOCKFORD
### PRIEST, 60

*She is the first woman to become reverend in the benefice and was born in the West Midlands, 'a long way from here. A completely different part of the country. A different character.' She was a teacher before and deals confidently with the secular world. No single reason led her to the priesthood: questions people asked her led to questions she began to ask herself; ideas arose from Bible readings; at one point there was a series of dreams. Then, while she was sitting at Christmas service one year, the phrase 'sheep without a shepherd' came to her, just popped into her head. She went through seventeen interviews in the process of ordination. The most demanding part of the selection conference was being observed all the time, not just in interviews but at mealtimes and while socializing. 'They're looking for people who haven't just got information in their heads,' she said. 'They're looking for people who can interact socially.'*

I started here on Shrove Tuesday in 2001. It was just at the time when the foot-and-mouth crisis began, so I was thrown right into it. I remember a local woman came up to me at the service where I was licensed and said, 'I think it would be a good idea to pray for the farmers.' I was very grateful for the tip, because

it certainly wasn't built into the service. We prayed for them.
And almost immediately we closed two of the churches, Hoo,
which is right next to a cattle farm, and Letheringham, which is
actually on farm land. We had to.

I am responsible for six villages, five churches. One of the
churches in Akenfield was closed in the 1970s. It is not an old
building compared to the others, which are medieval in origin;
it is, I think, a Victorian church. It was in a very bad state of dis-
repair and the decision was made to close it, which must have
caused a lot of heartbreak at the time. Various artefacts from the
church were supposed to go to other churches in this area: some
of the pews, for instance, and some communion silver as well.
The organ was supposed to go to Monewden, but there was a
lot of vandalism in the church when it was left empty. I think
the roof was in bad repair, so the organ never went to
Monewden.

We don't have any plans at the moment to close any of the
other churches as places of worship. There are some churches in
the diocese that probably have three services a year on special
occasions to keep the building alive. It's very difficult to know
when to close a church. I suppose there should be a level where
the congregation is so small, but then some of our congrega-
tions are already small.

Sometimes there will be five or six of us at the eight-thirty
communion; sometimes we get as many as twelve. I don't mind
if I'm just looking out at two or three people. I never mind. For
two reasons. Jesus told us that when two or three are gathered
in his name, he is there in their midst. And then there's that
wonderful sentence in the Book of Common Prayer, in the
Eucharistic prayer, which reminds us we are joining the worship of heaven. Therefore we are with angels and archangels
and all the company of heaven. So we are part of a much,
much larger congregation, even though there might only be a
handful of us out there in the pews. Churches have their peaks

and troughs and it may be that two or three people keep that church alive now, but in two years' time, three years, five years, ten years, there might be a completely different pattern in the population of that village and you might find that numbers will rise.

The nature of the populations in these villages is changing. The 1960s was a crucial time, when agriculture changed and the kind of people who lived in your villages changed. I looked through the baptism registers, the old ones that went back to the nineteenth century, and they showed that up until the 1960s the father's occupation, almost without exception, was farm worker. You might have had the postman or the woodsman, but 95 per cent were farm workers. Suddenly you get the change. You get British Telecom building its research station at Martlesham, which is between here and Ipswich. You get people moving in to take up jobs and looking for accommodation in the villages round about. People with an income move in so they can buy a couple of cottages and make them into one big house. It's the influx of professional people. You still have the residue of the agricultural population, particularly in Hoo, but you do get this change. In some of the villages, like Dallinghoo, there are a lot of young families. There is the potential there of drawing in a new congregation. Not to a service like Book of Common Prayer, or early-morning communion, because that's not what they're familiar with. They may not be familiar with any church service. So I try to get them to something which is family-orientated.

Church life and village life overlap much more in a village than in a town. Living in a village doesn't necessarily make people church attenders but it might draw them in to supporting the church in other ways. There are a lot of villagers who will arrange flowers, who do the cleaning. They'll go to fundraising events and even organize fund-raising events for the church. Because that's part of village life. But they might not necessarily come to church services, or they might come only when it's harvest or Christmas.

So for me, I have to make as much as I can with the services that draw in larger numbers. Mothering Sunday, for instance, is still very popular. In some urban areas it doesn't make sense any more, where you've got broken families. My husband's eldest son is a vicar in Stoke-on-Trent, which is one of the most deprived areas in Britain today. It's more difficult having a Mothering Sunday service in the traditional way in a place like that. But in the villages you can still build on the tradition. Mothering Sunday and harvest Sunday: if I do these services well, make them attractive and make people feel welcome, there will be the possibility of their coming again. You will find families bringing babies for baptism much more in the villages than you find in the town.

I am the first woman to hold this role in this benefice. It doesn't seem to have been a problem. Obviously that was one of the things the church wardens had to consider when I was asked to come and look at the job: would they be prepared to have a woman. It does create some problems in Akenfield because of the Baptist chapel. In that particular chapel there are people who cannot accept a woman's ministry. So it has meant working together with the Baptist chapel has not really been possible, which is sad. We have done what we can. For instance, remembrance services are usually held in the church because that's where the war memorial is. And so I've made sure, each of the years I've been here, that the sermon has been preached by a man. I took the service the first year and my husband preached. I took the service the second year and invited the Baptist pastor to preach. Last year my husband took the service and preached while I went to one of the other churches (that's another difficulty with remembrance: there are three services on at the same time and I can't be at all of them). This year I've invited the archdeacon to take the service and preach, and I shall be at Dallinghoo.

There is a verse in *2 Timothy* which says, 'I do not permit a woman to teach.' So the strict Baptists accept my teaching children, but not preaching in an adult congregation. That is a frustration and I somehow feel that if we were pulling together we might be a more effective witness in the village. Some of the people who are Akenfield villagers from way back, it doesn't bother them as much as some other people in the chapel.

There are some people who say they think a woman's better than a man, that women take that kind of service better than a man would. I don't think men or women are better than each other, we just have a complementary ministry. I think it's important we have both men and women ministers. You know, working together. I try wherever possible, in a service, to make sure there is a male voice as well as my own – one of the men doing one of the readings or helping to do the prayers, something like that. Because I don't want to give the impression that religion is only for women.

When I started here I was doing four services on a Sunday. The pattern I inherited was half-past eight, half-past nine, eleven o'clock, six-thirty. That meant I had no time to talk to people after the morning services.

I'd get up at half-past six. I'd just have time for breakfast. Usually I'd try to listen to the eight o'clock headlines before I left home. During my first year of being a curate at St Augustine's in Ipswich, Princess Diana died. I arrived for communion and the vicar said to me, 'Have you heard the news this morning?' I said no, and neither had most of the congregation. He had the job of breaking the news to them. So I never do a morning service now without having listened at seven or eight o'clock to the headlines.

I would get to the church at quarter-past eight. I don't have my own parking space but it isn't as though we've got great crowds fighting for space. After the service, no time to talk; I'd have to be somewhere else by half-past nine. So I'd shake hands, jump in the car, drive like the clappers. Usually I'd still keep my cassock alb on. I could time the journeys to the minute, so straight in, start the service at half-past nine. I gave the wardens instructions: if I am ever late for a service, give me five minutes; if I'm still not there, announce the first hymn and you can take the first part of the service on your own.

They could actually take it up to the reading of the Gospel, if necessary, if they used the 'we' and 'us' form of the absolution. Now, it never quite got to that, but I did sometimes arrive once the confession had started, or quite often I was processing up while they were singing the first hymn, rushing in. I would take a second to see how I looked, then off up the aisle. That service would end at half-past ten, which would give me a few minutes before I needed to be in Akenfield by eleven o'clock.

It was all so fast. I would have to leave conversations halfway through, and they would just see this white figure in a cassock alb rushing past. It was absolute nonsense. The church wardens could see the pastoral implications of changing the pattern of services so I could at least talk to people, some of whom I would not see for another month because that was their monthly service. The ten or fifteen minutes after a service is very important sometimes, especially with an elderly congregation.

I suppose there's still something of the old kind of faith around. It's different where you've got people who've lived elsewhere and have had experiences of other churches. But probably the traditional belief in a place like Akenfield is very similar to how it was years ago. It's a belief in God rather than in Jesus and the spirit. Maybe that's because it's rural and you get the sense of the creator God. So it's not a very trinitarian faith in some cases. And also because there are some people who have only ever worshipped in their own church here or in another church in the benefice. They aren't aware that there are other ways of doing things. I would like to broaden their experience and help them to see that what happens here isn't the only thing that has to happen. The question of music always comes up. People dislike what they consider to be 'happy-clappy' music. That's the actual phrase. I'd just like to help people to see that maybe there are one or two modern worship songs which are as good as if not better than some of the old-fashioned hymns we sing. I often get accused of choosing hymns that people don't know and I cannot believe they don't know them, but that's because my experience is much broader.

I think it may be a very rural thing. I've only got my experience to go on, but certainly in the town, if anything, it was a much more Jesus-based faith, because both churches I was associated with were much more evangelical and preached putting faith in Jesus quite regularly. The difference is being aware that Jesus is God. I think if you were to ask some people here they wouldn't think that he was. They would think of him as a good teacher, a miracle worker, but not God incarnate. The Holy Spirit doesn't always get that much of a look-in either because that can be a difficult intellectual concept, unless you've been taught it. So much safer to stick with God. We know about God: God the creator, God the one who provides the good earth and the rain and the sunshine.

## DON EWINGS
### HANDYMAN, 68

*Newcomers are jokingly warned to watch out for him because he will get them involved in village life – organizing fund-raising dinners, running meetings, even mowing lawns. He raises money for the village by applying for small grants and donations. Most days he can be seen in spattered overalls, having come from wrestling with bathroom fittings or chopping firewood. Thanks to Don's work, Akenfield has what he calls an 'I.T. hut' which is full of computers and he is expecting a photocopier to arrive soon – all donated. He's planned another hut on his own land to store the village's communal tables, chairs and lawnmower. The church lawn caused a stir at the last meeting, when at first no one would volunteer to mow it. Slowly, with Don gazing over his glasses, hands began to be raised.*

My family lived in a little road behind the Pears soap factory, which made that semi-transparent soap and stank like something awful. The smell filled the entire house. It was a cul-de-sac in Isleworth, just beside Heathrow Airport, with forty-eight houses. I was three when the war started, so really all my childhood was dictated by the war.

Because the Pears soap factory was being used to make munitions, about half our road was wiped out in the Blitz, although our house was never hit. Father was works manager at a firm that made precast concrete slabs, which meant we had the first prefabricated concrete air-raid shelter in our garden. That's where I spent most of my childhood. Our pastime every morning was to go out and retrieve lumps of shrapnel from fenceposts. Father was a volunteer fireman in the fire service, so he went down to the London docks during the Blitz. Mother was in the ARP, the civilian air-raid wardens, which meant I was brought up in the community because Mum and Dad were either out fighting fires or putting bombs away. Then a bomb took out my cousin's house, which was four doors away. Mother said, 'Right, that's enough.' We were evacuated to Hitcham, just outside Stowmarket, to my aunt's house.

They were only dropping bombs on London for a year, then it went to the mid-part of the war, where there weren't air raids. Instead, the flying bombs started appearing. We used to sit in the air-raid shelter watching the doodlebugs. They had a flame on the back, so you could see them coming over, and they were so crude that when they ran out of fuel the engine stopped, the flame went out and they fell to earth. If they went over the house, we were quite safe. If the light went out you ran like hell. One went out right over us, landed about half a mile away, and shook us out of bed. So it was off to Aunt Lizzie's again. I stayed there until after the war. Father was sent up to the Midlands to open a factory to make prefab housing for the bombed-out people. I stayed there, got married and was sent down to Ipswich, bought a house in Felixstowe and eventually I got divorced.

All I could afford was this little cottage. I bought it twenty-two years ago and it was totally derelict. There were no windows, no doors. Everything was boarded up. The stairs had gone and there was no running water, no electricity, no sewage, nothing. The piece of paper that came from the estate agent said at the top VIEW AT YOUR OWN RISK. And so I bought it and took it completely to pieces. All that was left was the oak frame, standing up like a skeleton. We subsequently found it was actually one cottage extended to two cottages. The one cottage this end is about 1500 and the other cottage the other end was originally a lean-to barn or cowshed that was put on in 1807.

Back when I moved here, the community wasn't as coherent as it is now. Nothing happened until a big snow storm in 1987. We were cut off for a week from the main road and no supplies could get through. There was, literally, eight foot of snow across the road. The farmer just across the fields had a herd of cows but the lorries couldn't get in to take his milk away so one snowy day he came across the field on his tractor with a churn of milk. He came right into the village and rang a bell.

We all wandered out to see what the kerfuffle was about. There's the old way of selling milk, where you have a pint or a two-pint measure. He scooped it out of the churn and into the jugs people had brought out from their houses. He gave his milk away because we hadn't got milk and he had too much. And everybody stood around and said, 'Oh, that's where you live, is it?'

# CYNTHIA HOWLETT
## SHOP ASSISTANT, 47

*She and her husband, Ed, were married in 1982 at Akenfield Church. They moved out of the village later that year. She wanted to live in Akenfield, where she had spent all her life, but the house prices were too high. They bought a terraced house in Ipswich and Ed fixed it up until they were able to buy a house in a village on the outskirts of Woodbridge. 'We're getting back to the country, slowly.' Today, at the home of her parents, Percy and Phyllis, in Akenfield, a fire is lit and a kettle is perched nearby to boil water for tea. Percy calls his wife Mother; Phyllis has a suitcase of fingerless gloves she has knitted to sell at local events. Ed sits in the chair near the sizzling fire. The only sound that comes from him is the flip of his newspaper until a topic of conversation catches his interest and he emerges from the slow pace of the Sunday afternoon to speak. 'When I first moved to Ipswich I talked to everybody,' Cynthia says. 'They thought I came from space. I hate it here, I used to say to Eddie. Then they got used to me. I was the only one saying "Morning" and "Evening", but then I was used to how people related to each other in Akenfield.'*

CYNTHIA: I started working in the village shop in 1974. It's the one that's now been converted to a house on The

Street. It was a proper village shop then: there was an old door with a brass knob, and a wooden floor, and when you'd walk in what faced you was the sweet counter. It was dark as Calcutta in there. The owner, Mr Turner, used to sit on a little seat in the back, and when you'd come in he'd get up, rubbing his hands.

We had everything in that shop. We had to have everything; we were the only shop in the village. There was quite a range of sweets: Peppermint Aeros, Mars bars, blackjacks, fruit salads. There was a Corona lemonade stand near the door. We had cheese in blocks – we used to cut it off using cheesewire. We had sides of bacon and we used to have to slice bacon up if somebody wanted streaky bacon. It would come in sides and we'd have to sort it out on the meat slicer. What a skill that was! There were big chunks of liver and we'd have to cut it up. The joints would come rolled, so they'd just say their size and we'd cut them with a big meat knife. The next bit of the store was the boutique, where we sold clothes, wool, bicycle tyres, rabbit food, paraffin.

ED: They had to be able to fulfil everyone's list. Someone would go in and say, 'Box of cornflakes, bottle of milk, half a dozen eggs. Bike tyre. Rabbit food. Paraffin.' Yes, yes, yes, yes, they'd say. Then the customer would go home happy. If there was one item the shop couldn't do, well, they might go somewhere else for everything.

CYNTHIA: There was one old boy used to come in and ask for paraffin when it was pitch-dark out. We kept it in a little cubbyhole, in a little shed outside, and I had to go out in the dark with a torch and get his paraffin for him. We sold necklaces and puzzles for children; we sold clothes. Somebody came round in a van who sold all different kinds of things and we'd go out to the van and choose what might go in the shop. We'd sell the *Star* and the 'Greenun', the football paper. On Saturday night the old boys would all be waiting for it to come in. We'd be trying to clear up, and they would all sit and congregate, waiting for it. The *East Anglian* employed someone to come round and deliver it to all the shops by van. You'd have to wait for all the results, so that was about six o'clock when that would come. We were open till seven. If it was a bit late you were there till half-seven. Or sometimes – ooh, and they weren't happy about this – we'd give up and say, 'We're shutting the shop, time to go home.' You've never seen a crowd of men more unhappy.

Some of the farmers would come flying down just when we were about to shut and we'd have to serve them. One farmer's family would come on their horses and say I want this, that and the other. They did it deliberately so they didn't have to queue up with other people. Working there, I got to know all the local characters. Some would come in just for the company. They'd come in every morning and get two things just so they'd see someone. I'd be the only person they'd see all day. They'd get bread, or a packet of fags, or a packet of biscuits. We'd have a receipt ready. One woman would walk all the way from Dallinghoo. She always used to call in and get an ice cream and treat us to one as well. We used to get her a receipt and she'd sit and eat her ice cream and talk to us. You had a character who would cut all the coupons out. She'd go in and buy all the things she could redeem. Must have spent all day cutting; she'd go around collecting the magazines.

ED: Whenever anyone would come in the shop, Cynthia would turn around and smile. 'Hello!' she'd say. A lot of people turn around and say, 'What do you want?'

CYNTHIA: I used to get phone calls when I was working, say, 'On your way home you wouldn't mind dropping by with

a bottle of gin, or a packet of my tea?' You get these old
ones saying, 'When you come past can you drop so and so
in?' And then you'll go in and they'll have this Camp
Coffee waiting for you. I hate Camp Coffee! There was a
little old man who would wait at the bottom of the drive
for me, he knew what time I'd go past. He'd wait for me
with a little brown paper bag full of cherry tomatoes. I used
to love eating them on their own, especially when they'd
just been picked.

ED: I remember the day I first blundered in there and saw her.
I was carting straw, working on my dinner time. I went in
there to buy a bottle of drink and bumped into Cynthia.

CYNTHIA: I asked him how to spell bananas.

ED: She was doing a sign to hang up. I'm the worst speller
ever. I said, 'Just spell *ba-na-nas*,' and I got a bottle of
Corona, a fizzy drink, and went.

CYNTHIA: And then he kept coming in!

ED: And every time I came in she was either on holiday, gone
out somewhere or delivering. So I said to myself, I think
she knows me and she's avoiding me.

CYNTHIA: I weren't avoiding, I was just out. I used to do
babysitting as well. I used to have Tuesday off, from one
o'clock onwards, and I used to do Boys' Brigade in the
evenings. I didn't have much time to myself, really. I
invited him to my twenty-first birthday party because I
knew his sister and he'd just lost his mum. He did call to
the door. Then he used to come and spend Saturday
evenings in the shop until I closed up.

ED: I used to sit in the back and take all the abuse from
Dolphie – that was short for Adolphus – who was one of
the old boys who hung around by the shop. He'd say, 'You
still riding around in that old stock car?' He'd be rude
about my car, see. I used to sit in the back with the heater
and talk about things with the old boys. When she was

done I would lift up her bike and put it in the back of the car.

CYNTHIA: I'd have to put the bread bin out. I'd be sweeping the floor, washing the floor, making everything else tidy, cleaning the meat counter. The meat would be all right, it would be put in the fridge. I'd have to get rid of any vegetables.

ED: Which was good for me because I got the mushrooms. They wouldn't be any good on Monday. I hardly ever bought any. I'd get a whole pallet full of mushrooms. I lived on those over the weekend. I kept on having lots of fry-ups with mushrooms. All these free mushrooms – lovely.

CYNTHIA: In the summers, I would go out for blackcurrants. Mr Peck – he was the orchard foreman then – he used to weigh the pail of blackcurrants and say, 'That ain't quite full enough, go back and fill it up.' He'd make sure we're doing it right so we're not just squashing things. If it were right, he would just put our number down. At the end of the summer, one week before I'd go back, we'd get our wage packet with our number on and how much was in it.

I'd have the radio on while I was picking – an old battery radio. We'd listen to Gary Glitter. We were allowed to have it on, we just weren't allowed to sit on the pails. Mr Peck used to come round and check us, and if we saw him coming we'd say, 'Here he comes, get off your pails.' If you didn't hear him come he'd say, 'Not allowed to sit on your pails.' Gary Glitter used to stick out; I remember him on there singing 'Come on, come on!' We used to sing along. We'd do a lot of singing and nattering, the big sky overhead. We used to pick hard, because the more we picked the more we earned. It was eight till eight we did, and it was good fun. We didn't think nothing about it. We wore a decent pair of shoes and old clothes. I can remember wearing a bright green jumper with these little crosses on it. I can see it to this day. No grass stains on our knees – because we sat on our pails! Some people brought stools along but the pails were just a little bit higher, level with the bushes, you see. The bottoms didn't fall out. We weren't heavy then, were we? We did respect Mr Peck. We didn't abuse his authority, it's just it was easier sitting on a pail.

CYNTHIA: A couple from out, from Ipswich or somewhere, bought the shop eventually. They'd never run a shop before in their life, certainly not a country shop. It went downhill fast. Not being funny, but country people do like to be respected and if you don't treat them the right way and be diplomatic you can very well upset them and they won't set foot in that shop any more.

    The former owner put a clause in to say that me and the other girl who worked there went with the shop. But the new owners didn't want us. They thought they knew best, but they knew nothing about shopkeeping. Mum's friend used to go in to buy things and to get her housekeeping cheque changed into cash at the shop. They started charging her for changing the cheque, so she didn't go any more, simple as that.

ED: When the former owners were there the shop was always lit up, bright, when you went past on a winter's eve. You could see it was a shop. When the new owners took over, it seemed they only had half the lights. One day I opened the door and went in. All I wanted was a packet of Polo mints, you see. I was waiting in the queue with these people, but a lot of the shelves seemed to be empty, not like it was before. I saw the Polo box up on the shelf. OK, he sells them, I thought, so I'll wait.

Eventually it was my turn to be served and I said, 'Can I just have a packet of Polos, please?' And he went and put his hand in the box and knocked the box around because it was empty. All that time waiting for a Polo and there was none in there! It's dark and dingy, you have to queue up for ages to get served, and then the one thing I did want — and it looks like he's got it — he ain't got none. I thought, You're not doing all that well, really. The next thing you know he's shut down, and I didn't wonder at that at all.

CYNTHIA: The last man who owned the shop just wasn't the kind of person who dealt with the public. If somebody said something out of context he'd jump back. In a place like that you got to take some of the stick people give you. You just have to absorb it and not throw it back. That's what happens when you work in a shop. Not everybody could be a shopkeeper — it's a talent. This man had never done that kind of thing before. You've got to learn if you want to keep the business. People would come in with their shopping orders. They'd say things like, 'I'd like my soap powder.' He hadn't got a clue what their soap powder was. There was also the incident with the Jif. There's two Jifs, you see — the cleaner and, you know, Jif lemon —

ED: For years the only Jif was this plastic little lemon with lemon juice in it. And the only time they really used to sell it was near Shrove Tuesday, pancake time. Then they brought out this white Ajaxy paste called Jif, see? One of the villagers came in and asked for Jif. The owner gave them the wrong one. He didn't know which one someone from the village might be looking for. We heard about it. 'The bathroom? Oh, the bathroom smells lovely, you know, but this creamy white stuff all over the pancakes was horrible.'

CYNTHIA: When the last people sold the place, they put a
   clause in that it shouldn't be used as a shop.
ED: As if they'd left a lot of trade behind.

## JACQUI LOMAS
### PRIMARY SCHOOL HEADTEACHER, 39

*She is a warm, authoritative presence, with Yorkshire lineage but she grew up and went to school in Holland. She is tall and deals directly with her staff and students. In the front office of the school a child is sitting with dampened paper towels on her knees. 'Right, then,' she says to her. 'Clare, are your knees going to fall off? If you stand up will your knees fall off?' The small blonde girl shakes her head. 'OK, then, why don't you throw your towels away and go play outside?' She does.*

I'm a teaching head, so I teach most of the week and I've got the youngest children in the school, which I love. The problem is, I get the same amount of paperwork as a non-teaching head would get.

We've got three classrooms. There are eleven computers for the children to use, and we're broadband now, since a couple of weeks ago. We're also going into a building programme to extend out, so the mobile is going, thankfully. It's a glorified shed, really. When I first came the youngest children were out there. What a great introduction: 'Welcome to school, we're going to put you in a shed.'

The positive side of a small rural school is children's social skills have to develop to quite a mature level quite quickly. They can't hide from problems. If they've fallen out with someone in their class or if they've fallen out with somebody in their year group there are not many children to choose from here. If you have a problem with one of your peers, you have to deal with it. In big schools some children don't ever have to deal with the emotional and social side of their own personal development. They can just move on to a different group: 'I've fallen out with these ones so I'll go and play over here.' Here you actually have to deal with it.

You'll often find that if children have a problem, we'll say, 'We do need to talk about this. Let's sit in the library and let's discuss it.' Some children find that a struggle. So I think the personal development is very strong in a small school and you have very different relationships with children – it's far more informal and it's far more personal, I think. We're with them all the time. We don't really have a staff room. We do have one, but . . . it's freezing in there. So at lunch times we sit down there with the children. We're always around, so the relationships are very different. You don't often hear raised voices here.

The downsides are the opportunities. We're a very small staff. I've tried to develop my touch-rugby skills but, you know . . . Instead of us doing touch rugby and football we get Big Richard to come in. And when he comes in we all fight – 'Oh, I'll do PE today.' 'No, I'll do PE today.' There are lots of companies out there that provide specialist PE support. This man, he does all sorts of different PE skills with our children and then he runs an after-school football club, where the parents pay for their children to come. So him teaching our PE lessons is like a perk.

I can teach netball, rounders, but I know my skills are quite limited, so we've also got a yoga teacher. My class have gone over to do yoga in the village hall right now. The teacher is a parent but she's a trained yoga teacher, so the class does yoga at our Celebration Assembly. The impact it has on young children is quite significant. They're all quite flexible little people.

We have a guitar teacher who comes in on a Tuesday morning. He's a peripatetic music teacher; we pay the county music service for his services. I've been doing singing with them – I'm not a music teacher – and I just brought in loads of CDs with prompts and they love that.

We've got a high percentage of children in such a small school with specific special needs. In my class we have a little girl starting who's got, you know . . . She's got problems. She's on the autistic spectrum. She was quite distressed in the corner at first but my class weren't fazed. When it's in a small school it's more nurturing anyway. There's certainly not a divide, no cliques. Children have their friends but you couldn't say that all children who have professional parents all play in one group and the others play in another. It's not like that at all.

You have to become the specialist for what the school needs. I'm not an early-years teacher – I trained to teach top juniors English – but I'm teaching four-, five-, six-year-olds at the moment. I think either you're a teacher or you're not. You have got those skills and you can learn the knowledge you've got to impart to children or you can't. I like that challenge. I think teaching the same thing – the French Revolution, say – year in and year out, I'd get really bored. It's never the same with young children.

There are a couple of children at the school who come from farming backgrounds but I would say their parents own the farm; they're more the affluent side. There aren't the farm workers' children because there aren't the farm workers any more. Most of the children who come to this school have parents who are professionals – they work at BT, work at the hospital. We've got lawyers' children. There's a wide spread of professional capacities within the parents.

There were rumours about the school closing down before I got here. It would be a private house if it wasn't a school and it would probably make a fortune because of the land and goodness knows what else. Someone would make a lot of money. For me, the school is an important part of this place. We're right across the road from the church. When there is a funeral we don't pull down the blinds. We discuss it. The children know. We'll say it's a funeral and they'll say, 'Do you think they're going to be buried in the churchyard?' And we'll have a discussion and say, 'Yes, maybe they are or maybe they're going to be cremated.' The older children definitely grasp the idea. We walk through the 'gravy-yard', as some of my kids say, every week. They'll stop and they'll say, 'What does that mean?' I think it's just part of this place, this community. I've always felt very uncomfortable saying to children, 'Oh, we don't talk about death. We don't talk about that.' Often the children will say, 'Look, those people over there are crying.' And I'll tell them, 'Well, you know, when people die it is really sad.'

We're forever out and about. We do things like litter picks. We use the village hall every week, we do our Christmas plays down there. We use the church for our services and lots of the community, especially elder members of the community, come in and join us. If you took the school out of this community, there would be another nice house, but there would be a huge gap. People in the community say that there's nothing better than being out pegging your washing and hearing the sound of kids in the distance, that shrill laughter.

MARTIN TILBURY and EMMA POWELL
MANAGERS OF THE THREE HORSESHOES PUB, 37 AND 34

*He looks like the publican he is, except for his goatee; she has red hair, an assertive laugh and an easy way of welcoming people into the room. They both smoke roll-ups. He drinks cup after cup of coffee behind the bar, occasionally scooting around to sit on one of the stools and light up, but returning to serve someone a drink. He concentrates when he pours.*

MARTIN: The name of my motorcycle club is the Black Shuck MCC. Black Shuck is an old legend of a so-called devil dog of East Anglia – *shuck* is an Old English word for dog. Truckers in America know all about the legend of the black dog. It goes right back to when the Vikings were coming over to Britain. They had dogs, deerhounds and the like, invariably dark in colour, and they were big, real big. As they settled down more, the dogs were left to roam and they tended to savage animals and occasionally people. As the dogs died off, the legend remained. In the days when smuggling was rife off the east coast, the smugglers took advantage of this legend that was very much alive. They would walk donkeys on the hillsides with candles on their heads like red eyes to scare the locals off so they could plunder a ship more or less undisturbed. Supposedly the

Black Shuck attacked Blythburgh and Beccles church 428 years ago this year, I think. Anyway, we were looking for a name that was representative of East Anglia. The fact it's a devil dog is irrelevant. We're not all a bunch of goatskin-clad devil worshippers pulling donkeys with candles.

When the club first started out it was known as the Spotted Cow, named after the pub where they met. They then changed their name because of unwanted interest from a biker club known at the time as the Outcasts, who have now amalgamated with a club called the Outlaws, who are worldwide. The Outcasts shut down the Spotted Cow, so the club at the Spotted Cow changed their name to West Ipswich. They changed venue but only achieved moderate success. The problem was that when they hosted an event only a few bikers turned out. Then someone observed that West Ipswich abbreviated to WI, Women's Institute. Not the best name for a bike club. So we changed our name to the Black Shuck and our events have been much, much more successful.

Black Shuck MCC is a social club for people who own motorbikes. For instance, one of the bikers was in last night. Fuzz was a friend before he was a member. Fuzz is his name, for reasons I don't even know. He's one of the longest-standing members. It's friendship with like-minded people. We just look after each other, help out. If someone hits upon hard times we all put a hand in our pockets and help out. We find there's a sort of honour among bikers. If you see a bike broken down, you stop and help. And I have been on the receiving end of that. About a week before my own crash, a guy I was sharing a house with crashed. He was knocked off. He hurt himself fairly badly, so our club had a collection. Because we shared a house it was my duty to bring that collection back to him. On the way home that night the lights on my bike failed and I put it through a fence with pig wire on it – four-inch-square wire. Bike slid through and punched a ten-foot hole in it.

EMMA: We're very glad the bike went first.

MARTIN: I couldn't afford to fix my bike. Fortunately all I suffered was a haematoma to my right leg and a concussion.

EMMA: But he wasn't coherent for two weeks.

MARTIN: It took ten days for me to hold a conversation.

EMMA: He'd get halfway through something and then just stop.

MARTIN: I crashed on the Wednesday and went to a motorbike rally on the weekend, but I just sat there in a daze. Couldn't drink – not for any medical reason, there was just no appetite for it. I think I managed to drink two pints in about twelve hours.

EMMA: Instead of twelve pints in two hours.

MARTIN: And when I finally decided to call it a night, I saw that getting into my tent was a problem. So I managed to unzip it and just fall over into the tent because I couldn't bend my leg. It was right around then things got serious with Emma. I think she started to take pity on me. We started flirting when she worked behind the bar at the Dog and Duck at Campsea Ashe, and it took off from there.

EMMA: Before that I had worked at a prison officers' social club down at Hollesley Bay. I started there as a casual, just helping out at functions behind the bar, and then worked up to actually running it. We had ten to twelve staff at the time, down to cleaners right up to deputy bar stewards. I ran that. Then we had a little falling-out. I walked into the Dog and Duck. The landlord was a friend of a friend. I said, 'Hello, Terry. Give us a job.' I said, 'I need at least sixteen hours a week.' He said, 'I don't know if I can offer you that on bar. Are you willing to learn kitchen?' 'Yeah, I'll learn kitchen.' It went from there. Basically I left on the

Friday night from one job and started the next one on the Saturday night. Then I met him.

MARTIN: Emma's dream was always to have a pub of her own.

EMMA: I think I was about five when I said I was going to have a pub. I did 'Mummy', 'Daddy', like normal children, but the words 'pub', 'chips' and 'church' came next. 'Church' – brilliant. 'Pub' and 'chips' – chips you can get away with, but pub? I was very young when I said I'm going to have one of those.

MARTIN: When we first laid eyes on this building, it was all 'Oh, wow! Oh, fantastic!' From the exterior we thought, What a lovely pub! Then we walked in and thought, What a ghastly pub! It was decorated pretty much as you'd expect to find a King's Road bistro – pale-beech furnishings, no wall furnishings, no history, which is very much a part of the traditional British pub. You need some history and it was all from IKEA. It was cold, it was stark. The quality of the beer was dubious to say the least and there was nothing to make you want to be there.

So we said, that's not for us. 'Cause we were already looking at another pub. Then things started to go pear-shaped with the other building and we pulled out of the deal. We spoke to a friend of ours who knew about the place and he said, 'Why don't you have another look?' We looked again and decided maybe we needed to speak to the owner to see if we could change it, which we did. He was in full agreement with us. He said, 'I personally like it, but it's in the wrong place so do what you feel you need to do to make it a successful pub,' which is what we've done. We've changed the furniture, introduced photographs and pictures on the walls and shelves with little bits of trivial junk to generate interest. He's been in since and he likes what we've done. The locals are very supportive of it.

EMMA: We did spend every Monday religiously at the market

for the old bottles, that kind of thing. We have three original Carlsberg crates.

MARTIN: Normally you inherit your pub's history. We've had to start from scratch. We've had to create the feeling of oldness and it's a lot harder than you think, because you think of something and don't really know how it's going to work until it's done. And then your taste might not be the same as the customers'. You're trying to build a feel.

EMMA: We totally painted throughout, but didn't get time to do the back hall. The bathrooms got done, the bar area got done. We had a private party and invited the whole village and friends and family. We opened at five-thirty on a Friday; we were still finishing painting at four. It was a mad panic.

MARTIN: The car park was packed!

EMMA: We didn't know what the food was like here prior. All we knew was it was way above what we wanted to do price-wise, and you're talking drizzled stuff and little bits of . . . Our biggest seller is shepherd's pie. Lasagne also goes mad. I can't physically keep up with it. That's why it's only on the specials board. We've only had two couples come in, look at the menu and say, 'Sorry, that's not for us.'

MARTIN: There would have been some customers who liked what was here and were bound to return. When they did they were going to get a bit of a shock. When people phoned up to make reservations we had to make a snap decision as to whether they were coming for us or for the previous place. If we thought they were from the last chapter of the pub's history, we tried to explain to them on the phone that we were under new management and it's very different to what it was. But that stopped very quickly.

EMMA: We moved in on a Saturday and my youngest started school in the village on the Monday.

'Oh, I hear you're the new landlady,' other parents

would say when I came to pick him up. 'Will you be a proper pub?'

'Yes, we're going back to being a proper country pub.'

'Wonderful. Will you have proper food at sensible prices?'

'Yes, no fancy food.'

Opening night was a baptism of fire. The next night two bike clubs decided to have a rideout to us. They said, 'We're all coming out on Sunday. Get the roast on.' We had thirty bikes in the car park. It can be quite intimidating for people who don't know what biker clubs are about to think, 'Oh, my God, look at all those leather-clad bikers. That's scary, we can't really go there.' We did worry. But we've actually had villagers say, 'When are the bikers coming down next? Cracking night!'

MARTIN: One of our chaps who comes in, he came in from work in a full business suit. Quite a big lad, I'm sure he wouldn't be easily intimidated. He said, 'Great. When are they coming again?' They bring life into the place. And I think that's what they like. A couple of regulars pulled up and said, 'I don't know if I should go in.' They did and once they were in they thought the atmosphere was so good that any reservations they had were dispelled there and then. They stayed for the session, had lunch here, loved it. It had an atmosphere. The lads in the club, they don't just keep themselves to themselves. They talk to other people, so nobody feels displaced by them. So it does work quite well. It's not a biker atmosphere.

Most members of the club drink coffee. You'll see this great big biker head up to the bar and ask for a pint of Coke. We're social people, we'll talk to people whether we're the landlord or the customer. If that's your nature, then doing that as part of your job comes very easily. If people come in and they're a little bit timid, you greet them in, ask them where they're from. If they're on a bike, ask them what they're riding.

There's nothing here for people who get into trouble in towns: no fruit machine, no TVs, no loud music, no modern music. I think you could call it rock and pop over the last thirty years. They're all compilations, so there are no particular artists. I don't put them together. They're bought ones. I don't have the time. We tailor it to who's in. If we've got a younger crowd I'll put the more modern one on and if they're older I'll put the 1960s stuff on. They sit here and they love it. Sometimes they'll break into song. It's always at a volume where you can have a conversation. We've got to be mindful of the people eating at the other bar. They don't want to be drowned out.

We've got farmers, builders, solicitors, accountants, BT technicians and engineers – people from all walks of life. When you're a landlord you've got to be able to walk every walk of life and talk to your graduate professionals and your manual workers. That's what helps you generate an old-pub feel. When you get customers like that in, it generates an atmosphere. There's only so much you can do to make the pub look nice but that doesn't in itself create atmosphere. You need people in to get that. And we're now starting to get them in. Sunday afternoon is feeling like pubs did years ago.

*Farming II: 'Who's the Mug, Really?'*

## CHRIS GREEN
### DAIRY FARMER, 41

*He is wearing a dark blue corduroy shirt and jeans. He has a few lines on his face but they're etched into places that suggest laughter rather than worry. We're sitting in his kitchen. Last Saturday, Chris and his partner, Jane, decided to tear down the ceiling. The beams are showing. There's piping exposed. We sit down to a meal of chilli and a baked potato and Chris talks instead of eating. He always does this, he says, and ends up with a plate of cold food afterwards.*

I left school in Akenfield in 1980. I didn't excel, not really. I was quite a stupid pupil, I guess, except for physics. I was top in physics, but I dropped it at fourteen because the mix of subjects meant I had to do German and I didn't want to do that. So I dropped it to do cookery, which wasn't like proper cooking – it was just 'go there for half an hour and shut up' kind of cooking. So I decided to jack in the only subject I was any good at because it didn't suit the way I wanted to live. Nowadays, parents wouldn't let a child do that. My parents didn't let me do everything I wanted, but they certainly let me make my own decisions. If you wanted to make a fool of yourself, well, it's your life, idiot.

When you're young you just sit there thinking, What should

I do? Quite like to be a footballer. I was all right at football, but
I knew I wasn't good enough. I played in a band at school. With
music it was patently obvious to everyone I wasn't good enough,
but it wasn't obvious to me. So I was unemployed. Right about
1980 in England there was quite a lot of unemployment.
Thatcher was in and it was a turbulent time, so being unemployed then was quite common, particularly for school leavers.
Also, being disillusioned was in fashion because the punk thing
had been going on, so to profess to be a toilet cleaner was a
badge of honour. 'I've got a really crap job.' 'Hey, I'm very
impressed.' Punk was dead funny, really. Unless you were in the
Clash, it was just quite funny.

Punk made it to Akenfield, in fact. Not in the sense that it
made an impact in our society. There were some people who
didn't like their parents, but there wasn't a massive movement to
smash the state. Because it's England – we do a hell of a lot of
posturing but we don't ever get round to sorting things out.
We've still got the Queen, after all.

Still, we had a few people walking around with mohicans. It
was the fashion of the time, but I don't know if there were any
fully-fledged anarchists. I don't even think Johnny Rotten
bought into 'Anarchy in the UK'. It was just a good old song
title. I remember seeing one or two bands in Ipswich, punk
bands, and they were great because they were so lively. Everyone
was pogoing and that sort of stuff. It was just dead funny.
What's the 'no future' song by the Sex Pistols, 'God Save the
Queen'? One punk band from Woodbridge, I can't remember
their name – they weren't that good – but I remember they used
to play at the Sea Scout hut down by the river. I remember
them singing the 'no future' bit and they were all really nice
enough blokes who liked music. I knew one of them vaguely. I
don't think they'd ever slept rough. I dare say they're all doctors
and solicitors now. I don't think I knew a true solid punk
around here who really bought into the nihilism. It would be

hard to be a rural nihilist. Life is too good! You know, you walk out and see the birds flying in the sky, the trees swaying in the breeze and think, Anarchy, what?

Eventually I went to college at Portsmouth Polytechnic. I attended a few lectures, played a lot of cards. I get up for work at about half-four now and don't bat an eyelid, but back in those heady days nine o'clock was quite a stretch. I honestly don't know what I did. I only stayed a year before coming back to Akenfield.

Farming was not very high on my list back then. Not very high at all. I sort of fell into a job at my father's dairy farm. They didn't really need me when I came back, there was another bloke working. But he died when he was still young, thirty or thirty-one. Maybe if he hadn't died it might have been different. He just had a heart attack. A dramatic stop, and after that I was required. I still work with my father now.

The way our parlour works is we have five cows come in either side. You milk one side and while they're being milked by the machines you clean the next five, and as one finishes, you substitute another. Once this side is all done, they go out of a gate and the next five come in. And it just goes from one side to the other, really. It's called a herringbone parlour, one oblong-shaped building with cows on either side. It's a relatively old system. We've had the parlour since the 1970s but it works well. The mainframe is probably the only original bit left. I expect every bit has been changed, every little piece.

Most farms were set up around families, but that's gone. My grandad hardly milked a cow in his life. Instead, he was the one who bought and sold cattle all the time. With that money he bought this farm and my dad ran the cows. My dad now buys and sells cattle and I look after the cows with my uncle. We've managed to survive. We have a great . . . I mean, we have a good life. But you couldn't financially start a farm up now and make a profit out of it. The land costs too much and the houses cost too much and the returns, the returns are just about good enough to warrant doing it but not to leap into it. The only kind of people buying land now are people coming from other businesses, just rolling money over or wanting to do something else if they're rich enough.

To set up even a dairy farm of our size – we've got about 140 cows – you'd need a million and a half pounds. Land is two and a half thousand pounds an acre, and you'd need 200 acres. That's half a million at least to buy the land, and then you got to buy the animals. If you wanted just 100 cows that would be 500 pounds each, so there's another 50,000 pounds. Then all the equipment. I suppose you could buy a dairy farm with the facilities, but you'd obviously have to pay for those as part of the deal.

A lot of the farms around here are gone because they've all amalgamated. Most of the land in this area is farmed by about four or five businesses now. Now, if you're in arable – we're dairy – but if you're in arable, each man is supposed to work 500 acres on his own. Obviously not with a spade and a fork – the equipment's improved so much. In 1974 500 acres would have been a big farm.

It's all about insurance now. When I was a child, no one was concerned about getting hurt; there was always someone riding a motorbike across a field. Now the school has closed the adventure playground because – I don't know, the ground's too hard or something. It's the insurance. Everyone's got to second-guess what could go wrong. It's the same with the farm. For our dairy contract we have to have contingency plans for almost any eventuality. I remember one of the questions I got asked by the guy who came around was, 'What happens in a fire?'

'Well, we call the fire brigade,' I said. 'What do you expect?'

He said, 'Where's your appointed assembly point? Where do you assemble if there is a fire?'

'Well, we assemble where the fire is and we have a look at it. I don't know.'

He said, 'You do need an official assembly point.'

'It's around this table,' I told him.

He said, 'That's OK.'

That was his box ticked. For us to have a contract with him we had to have a flood plan, hurricane plan, all these stupid things. 'If all your buildings blew down where would you house your cows?' Good question! Assuming my own house has blown down, I've got larger priorities than the bleeding cows! I'd just let them out in the field. But they'll say, 'That's not right, they haven't got shelter.' I just think, God, give us a break. Eventually you get to some sort of compromise. I think we are going to erect buildings out of Heston square bales. That's the contingency plan if all the buildings get blown down. I have no idea what will really happen, but that's what written on our dairy contract.

I don't know if there is a great future for agriculture in England. I hope there is, because it's a nice life. But we're never going to be able to compete with the Ukraine and Poland. Well, until Poland gets richer. If you were going to put agriculture in any particular part of the world, you wouldn't put it in England.

I know a lot of people moan about subsidies, and quite rightly too. It's ridiculous that we get paid money for just having fields. But we get quite good subsidies because we get such bad prices. Our milk is sold, as of this month, at about eighteen and a half pence per litre, and that, at best, is round about the cost of production. If you count all your costs you're lucky to produce milk at eighteen pence. To keep in business you need subsidies.

There's a new subsidy coming in from a more environmental point of view. We're going to get sixty pence for every metre of hedge and ditch we've got. Quite honestly, that's ridiculous.

You read it and think, Blimey, that's quite good, because we've got a lot of hedges and ditches. But that's beside the point. You feel almost obliged to meet all the regulations because there is so much money coming. It's daft but we have to have it, because ultimately the likes of Wal-Mart and Tesco are not worried at all about us. They want the supply and that's all they care about. We sell to a Footsie 250 company, quite large, and even they can't go to Tesco and Wal-Mart and drive a bargain. They still have to take the price and as a consequence the guy at the bottom of the chain, which is us, eventually takes the hit. And because we take the hit we have to take the subsidy, which comes off the taxpayer.

Food is relatively cheap and people don't appreciate that. If you didn't have the supermarket stitching us up in the first place it would all work the other way around: people would have to pay less tax because they wouldn't have to subsidize us. But that's how it is. As a result, I don't think farmers are particularly popular. I can understand it, though. If I had a tough job, you know, working in a call centre and getting paid 12–15,000 pounds a year and I was aware how much subsidy was going to agriculture – and it's enormous, the actual numbers are phenomenal – I would resent it. I would just see the number and think it's going straight into someone's pocket as profit. That isn't the case, but I would feel kind of resentful if I was, you know, not having a great time answering phones.

Most of the farmers I know live in nice houses and we've all got bleedin' big gardens. Certainly more than 50 per cent live, if not on big incomes, then in houses that are better than the average. I couldn't afford to buy this house on what I earn. In the real world, on what we actually make, you couldn't have this house. That's why we're the only farmers left in a house like this. Most sell up because the money's too good.

People who move out to the country start to realize that

farmers do farm. They find out it is a kind of business. Then they throw it back in your face and say, 'It's not a business because you get subsidized, you know.' I accept we get subsidized, but so does nearly every other business in a roundabout way. The nuclear power industry is subsidized, all the transport systems are subsidized. Anybody who works for the government has a subsidized pension. But we're the ones who get the most obvious subsidies.

If you've got two products at the same price, people will tend to buy local ahead of foreign. But the problem is, most people buy on price. I buy as much British stuff as I can. I like to buy as much Brit machinery as I can, but there are some things we can't get here. Having said that, we've got a Daihatsu four-track, four-wheel drive because it's quite a lot cheaper than a Land Rover Discovery. It's quite British, isn't it? I mean, if you wanted a four-wheel drive to drive around Mayfair you wouldn't buy a Daihatsu. But if you wanted something to pull a trailer – well, there's nothing wrong with Discoveries but on price, you know, as a business option, in our opinion, Daihatsu's a better option. The guys in Korea, they're doing a good job on that one.

People expect things to stay the same, particularly people who come to or retire to a village with a dream of what village life is like. They put up with a lot of smells from us, we're quite a good thing from their point of view; it makes their houses worth more money. The bigger houses in the press – somehow they always manage to snap a picture with a cow munching grass somewhere near them. It's ye olde England.

But with all these people moving to the countryside comes a blandness, a sort of sameyness about everything. Most of the new houses seem the same. Everybody talks about property now because it's worth so much money, but when we were kids I should think in Akenfield there were at least five or six empty, derelict places, and they were big houses. They were nice houses. When people moved, sometimes there was nobody to move in for a while. These derelict houses were all different, all in a different state of repair, so you knew one from another, whereas most of the new houses that go up are the same, or similar. There's nothing wrong with them, but they could be anywhere.

There was one house in Akenfield that had a big thatched barn in front of it, a massive barn which now would be developed. The guy who owned it back then just bulldozed it down because it was in the way. It was in a hell of a state but now it would be 150,000 pounds of potential for someone to come along and buy. The people moving out here from the city – people with money, this is – buy their nice detached farmhouse and they always try to put a paddock next to it. You see it around here: people buy the house and then they buy about ten or twenty acres around it. They like their own little piece of England, they want to have a few lambs or a cow or a goat. Great. It is a nice thing. The problem with it is it costs quite a lot to do this as a hobby, assuming you've got another job. It's quite time-consuming. In the last few years we often get offered pieces of grass just to cut for hay – ten acres here, ten acres there – because people don't know what to do with it. Ten acres is quite a hell of a garden! If you've got to keep these ten acres clear, and get your hedges cut, and your ditches dug out, it's quite an expensive hobby.

Sometimes you slightly smirk. I can see why they do it, but you don't need ten acres to live the dream. Around here, I should say there's probably eight farmhouses and this is the only full-time farm business. I'm not saying they all were when I was a child, but certainly five or six would have had a farmer in them. There's one particular cottage in the village, up the road. It used to be a little farm worker's cottage and it was bought by . . . well, it's been bought by someone from away. It used to be called a 'cottage'; it's now called a 'hall'. And they've put an extension on it and they've put a field with it, planted a few trees. Every tradesman in the area has absolutely stitched them up. They've had the drive done about three times. Everybody can see they spend money like water. They changed the name of the house from 'cottage' to 'hall', and people went *cha-ching*. They obviously want to be lord of the manor, so they can pay for the privilege, I guess.

It's the same with a lot of these houses that are bought by people who come down for the weekend. There's been a boom for gardeners, or specifically for guys just setting up businesses to go around cutting lawns. There's almost an unwritten law that if it's a local you charge X and if it's a weekend person you charge Y. There is a slight undercurrent of 'you can stitch them up because they don't really live here'.

Farming is nice because it's simple. It's too simple for some people; a lot of people like things to be a bit more complicated. But I like it. We've got cows: you feed them and they give milk. Once a year they have a baby calf. And that, for all the technical jargon you read in the press, is about as far as it goes. It's not as boring as that sounds. I wouldn't have ever believed I would end up doing it. When you actually analyse it, it's like, Why on earth would anyone do it? But tonight, for instance, we've got two cows in the shed which will probably calve. I like calving cows, to see the calves flap their ears and stagger up. I'm not saying you stay out there every night to watch them do this, but just occasionally, if the moment is right, you see these things that are born! In fifteen minutes' time they try to get up. It is remarkable and it doesn't stop being remarkable, you know. A lot of the time you're too busy to take notice of it, but if you have got the time to sit back and see this thing just sort of lying there get up and walk within the hour – it is a miracle. It's more of a miracle than a lot of the miracles of technology we have. They're wet and covered in afterbirth, but their mothers lick them clean. They look weak and vulnerable, they look like Bambi, they're all legs. But you don't as a rule take any notice of it, because it's just work.

I think these are the best days of my life. I'm in my prime, like Miss Jean Brodie. I know every . . . well, not every blade of grass, but I know the land very well. It's just dirt, but it's what I see every day. This is one of the great privileges of doing what farmers do. You've got a hell of a lot more of the planet than most people.

# JOE EMENY
## FORMER FARM WORKER, 79

*He has been shaped by his years on the farm: short and stout, broad-backed and barrel-chested. He punctuates his conversation with a low, mischievous chuckle. Old Joe, some of the villagers say, he's a real storyteller. We sit in his council flat, surrounded by mementoes from the past, including photographs of some old friends. 'Girls never got nicknames back then,' he says, but the men did. Dodger – 'Playing football he would always go in and out of everyone.' Stoat – 'He was a gamekeeper.' Giner – 'I've got no idea where that came from.' And what was his? Shortie, he says and chuckles – 'I wonder why they chose that?'*

I was born in 1925 in Essex, in Stanway, not far from the zoo. I wasn't born in the zoo, not quite. Ha ha. My mother lost her husband when I was two years old, and she moved to Akenfield with another man and me. So I've been here nearly eighty years.

All my life I worked on a farm. I went to school at Dallinghoo until I was eleven, then I went to Wickham Market, but I left when I was thirteen. My birthday came in the Easter holiday and we was allowed to leave at fourteen then. I went straight on to the farm the next day. It was on a Wednesday. I came home from school on the Tuesday and told my mother I'd

finished school. She said, 'You've got to work tomorrow then.'
When I first got there the old farmer he said, 'Boy, you'll have
to do what I tell you. You know that, don't you?' I said, 'Yes.' So
he told me to get in the kitchen and start scrubbing the kitchen
floor. I was what they used to call a backus boy. I cut the kin-
dling, lit the old brick oven and cleaned the shoes. Then I went
to cowman. There's always two cowmen, and one of them left,
so the old farmer said, 'Boy, I think you'd better have a go at
that. You've got good strong wrists.'

When I first started as a cowman I used to have to milk the
cows by hand every morning and every afternoon. I'd get up at
quarter to five. I lived in them houses, council houses, just
down the road, so all I had to do was walk across the road early
in the morning. I was told I was very good. What makes a good
cowman, you might ask? Well, it's those strong wrists. The old
boy what showed me how to milk, George Mead, said to me,
'Boy, you're a darn sight better milking than I am.' When I finished milking a cow there'd be a few inches of froth on the top.
That's a skill, that is. You didn't have to work fast, you just had
to keep at it. As you come down on the cow's teats you just
nipped it, then let go, back up, nipped it again. There was nothing to it, really. I enjoyed it. You didn't think of much while you
were milking. You were just thinking, I hope that cow don't
bring his foot up! I been knocked over many times. Right into
the gutter. I wouldn't like to tell you what I say to the cow after
that.

George Mead used to live in the village but he finished up in
the home in Wickham Market. He died a couple of years ago,
but he was a real good farm worker. He taught me everything I
knew. He was a very small chap, but very agile, and he had a
very long pointed nose. He was a wonderful man. He'd do anything for anybody, he really would. I got on well with him.
When I went into the cowshed he would say, 'Boy, get a stool
then.' I got a three-legged stool, sat beside the cow and he said,

'Go like this.' And it came to me just like that. He couldn't believe it.

When I first heard of the milking machines, I thought to myself, That's going to do somebody out of a job. Fortunately I was the one who had to use it. They were what they call Simplex milkers and they came and demonstrated. The farmer I was working for then said, 'Joe, I want you to use them.' All I had to do was walk under the cow, put the machine on the teats, stand back. I missed using my hands. But I used to watch the old milk go up the tube, along the pipes and down into the churns. That was wonderful. And then after we done the milking we used to go in the dairy in the house and turn the bloody old butter churn for about an hour. I was turning it one day, a wooden one, and the lid flew off and all the butter went up on the ceiling. That was the farmer's wife who was there then, but she was a true Christian so she never swore. 'Oh, butter', that's just what she did say, honestly.

We used to plough all the land with horses, one furrow at a time. Now they have about eight furrows on a tractor. I think they were more skilled in those days than they are now. A lot. When you were ploughing you tried to keep it dead straight, but now when they plough they just go as the hedge goes. I mean, when the tractors and that first came out they used to plough round and round. They'd start in the middle and go round and round. It didn't drain so well. If you ploughed straight across and we got a lot of rain that would drain down the furrows. They used to have six horses on that farm and when you get three pairs of horses in a field ploughing it looks wonderful.

They were lovely Suffolk punches. They really were muscular. I remember when harvest came, we had a binder then – you know, what goes around and throws it out in sheaves? When you used to go around and pick it up, stand it up – what they call shocking – sometimes the corn would be full of thistles, and you can imagine what that was like picking them up. And then loading it up on to the wagon, taking it home and putting it on a stack. One day I was doing the stack and I got up to that height and the whole damn side slid out. That was a real skilled job, that was. Because if you got out a bit further than you should do, it would just go down. And then the bailers come in, so it's less work.

I think the best change was the combines. Look at the handling that saved; that was a lot of hard work. When it was in sacks you used to have to carry it up to the granary – twenty stone at a time on your back and when you got to the top of the granary steps you knew it. You'd tip it into a hopper, go down into the shed below it, start up the old mill, grind it up. I think there were twelve or thirteen steps, and you'd be carrying twenty stone a time. But I'll tell you what, though I shouldn't say it, I was as strong as an ox when I was younger, I really was. That weren't a lot of weight to carry then. I mean, that's only two and a half hundredweight. You used to take a horse and carry six sacks at a time, so you had six to take up and then you'd go back to where they were threshing it, get six more and up again.

The worst job on the farm in them days was when the old threshing engine came in. You had all the corn stacked up in stacks, or stooks as they called them, and when the threshing engine came in it used to pull between two stacks and you had to chuck the stuff down into the drum and thresh. The dust was unbearable, filthy. You used to go home at night, have a bath and go straight to bed, tired out. When I first learned to plough, I had a tractor with no cover on it. Your skin gets filthy, really black, especially if you were threshing beans. A lot of it was thistledown and that's all creepy-crawly. It used to craze you. It would get everywhere. You know the beans they grew for the cattle? God, they were absolutely black. You couldn't see across the stackyard, you couldn't see for dust. You had to strip off every day.

There were little tiny combines what you had to pull with a tractor and they came in about '45, just after the war. But they were very small. Now they've got fourteen-footers, haven't they? The first combine that come out, they used to bag it up and throw it on the field and you'd got to go and pick it up, take it back to the farm. When I saw those big combines I thought, I wish I was younger.

*We are riding in his tractor on an overcast autumn day, drilling wheat into the soil of a field in long passes. He wears overalls and operates the machine with an offhand ease. His voice lifts with excitement at the mention of his collection of steam engines. The enclosed cab of the tractor is hot but not uncomfortable; loud but not unbearable. A panel of electronic controls is at his right hand, and there are speakers around the cab. At the bottom of the field, he presses a button to make the tractor lift its drill and then he turns the machine in a slow, graceful motion, practised over the course of many autumns.*

I've been into farming since . . . well, I did day-release from school so I could farm. I always enjoyed it. The first word I said was 'tractor'. I suppose I looked out of the window and there was a tractor going past where I used to live. I've always worked on farms. The first one I worked on was a 1,000-acre farm with twelve of us working it. They also had a manager, and then the manager turned into a working manager so they needed one less person. I was last one in, first to go. I went on to another farm and the same thing happened: last in, first to go. By the time I got here I had been made redundant five times. You had ten blokes on each farm, but suddenly farms were merging and you had two blokes on two farms. It never cost much to get rid of me. 'Oh, so you've been here three years? Here's three weeks' pay.' That was at the massive amount of three or four quid an hour. Now we've got ten farms to look after. There's three of us out today, and that's a lot. Normally it's just me. Quite often it's just me out in the fields.

I work on the farm 100 hours a week just so I can keep going – and, well, I've got a Ferrari at home . . . Oh no! You had so much sympathy and now I've gone and blown it! But no, listen, it's an old Ferrari. I bought it in bits and I'm doing it up. I've got to be careful: I've got a five-year-old daughter and a six-month-old boy and I've got a place worth 300,000. Oh, you're losing sympathy for me again! But we bought it for 40,000 pounds eight years ago. Farm workers have to be good at doing everything, so I gutted it, stripped it. I done the whole lot myself. I'm just a logical bloke: if I see someone mix up a bit of cement or lay a few bricks I can do it after watching them for a quarter of an hour. That's the only way I've been able to get along in life.

I was never a drinker or smoker, and I've always saved money. Everyone says I'm tight; I'm not tight, I'm just careful. I don't see the point of spending money when you haven't got it. We haven't done any holidaying. Our devotion has been to get our house round and we spend all our time on that. Eleven o'clock at night and the wife is out there with a tractor with a cement mixer on the back. I'm laying bricks. The floodlights are on. You have to just work. This is what we did while we were young. Now we've got the place round and I've decided to put an extension on because we thought we might have two kids instead of just one. We doubled the size of the property. I dug all the footings up myself, rigged it up, put the windows in, did all the roof. I would say to her, 'Right, wife, the tractor's out there. You know how to start it.'

When I started farming every tractor had a different implement on it. You'd have a tractor on the rows, you'd have a tractor on the harrow, the plough and so on. Now this big tractor has to have narrow wheels for ploughing, but it's got wide tyres for drilling. It's got to double up and do the ploughing and the drilling and the rolling. It's got to be versatile to do everything. That's the whole thing – you've got to get an expensive tractor that will cover all the jobs now. You can't afford to have one tractor for each implement and one bloke on each tractor. It's just progress, apparently.

I used to drive all those old machines. My first combine never had a cab on it. The dust came off the front rail and headed straight to where I was sitting on the platform. I would get covered in the thick dust all day long, so I'd had to have a helmet with a hairdryer in the back to blow filtered air in. The bearings on the hairdryer helmet were squeaking all day; it was horrible. I used to sit on the top of the tank of the combine where the grain was collecting and steer with my feet so I was out of the dust. I'd drive like that all day. It used to be nice when it got pitch-black because there were no lights on the combine. You've got the moonlight. The dust level is down because it's just that little tiny bit damper. I've been out many a moonlit night, total black apart from the moon, going up and down on the combine. Someone knows you're there but they don't know your whereabouts. And you're just driving with your feet.

It's definitely better these days. Just look at the comforts you've got in here. Four speakers and your head is in the middle of all four of them when you've got the stereo on. You've got all the mod cons in here with you. It's refined really. It's nice to drive, nice to handle. It is the best tractor on the market as far as I'm concerned, and I've driven hundreds upon hundreds of tractors. It's slightly noisier than some, but it's nice to have the creature comforts built into your armrest. The steering is light.

With some of them it's so light you have to turn it three times just to get somewhere. I've only got to turn this one once.

I've been working on this farm for ten, twelve years. I've done about twenty different qualifications. I'm not saying I learned anything; the whole point of the training was to pass the tests, to get the certificates. I've got farm management, which I've never used; farm accounts; mechanized farming 1 and 2 and 3. It was interesting and it passed the time away in the winter. I've got craftsman's degrees in ploughing and combining and drilling and in spraying and fertilizing and basic tractor handling and tractor maintenance. You have to have fairly serious qualifications for handling the sprayer now, which is a good thing because any idiot could just go in there and chuck chemicals about that would eventually wash down the river.

We had a student come and help us on the farm one year. We had a big fifteen-ton trailer and he went roaring down the road three miles to the farm, tipped the trailer up in the yard, came roaring back to the field.

I was on the combine and I said to him, 'Why's your trailer still up?'

'Oh, shit,' he says, 'I forgot to put it down.'

Well, it's all well and good, but every single telephone line from here to Monewden was off-air because he'd taken all the lines out when he left the trailer tipped up. In the olden days they used to have loads of students who could jump on a tractor, roar about. It don't matter if they spill a bit, it wasn't worth a lot. You know, the profit margin was different. I used to work on places where they'd have a few students and oh, they'd break a few things and they'd forget to shut the tail gate on the trailer and the wheat'd be coming out. But you got through. The students made a bit of money. Now, with a 90,000-pound tractor, you can't afford to have a student near it.

The boss would probably say, 'This tractor is too expensive, it's got too many luxuries.' But I spend more time in here than I ever do at home. I'm in here fifteen to seventeen hours a day for months. Tractors are very hot things to sit in, so I've got the air conditioning on every day of the year, more or less. The cabs have got it all now. You'd think, Why do you want to have electric mirrors on tractors? Well, you try to reach that from the ground. And when you get really, really tired, the air conditioning keeps you on your toes. It keeps you going all night. That and the amateur radio – at about four o'clock in the morning the Australians and the New Zealanders come awake and we have a chat. That boosts me a bit too. I've been interested in CB radio since I was sixteen. I've had them in tractors for years – ever since the tractor was quiet enough to hear it. It used to be a nice community of farm workers on the CB and they were all in the fields. We'd chat among each other and have a laugh and have a joke all day long. But now we're so far apart you can't get to each other with a CB. That's why I've got the amateur radio. There's a chap in Kent – well, he's been made redundant in the past year, but I used to talk to him every single year, combine to combine, tractor to tractor. I used to tell him I had a better tractor than he did. But he had a better combine than mine, so it was one-all. It was nice to see what they were up to, what was going on. They've got different soil textures down there. It's lighter land in Kent – God's Garden or whatever they say. They could get their land all drilled up way before we could even think about it; ours was too tough to deal with a lot of the time.

I enjoy handling big machinery. It's always an unknown quantity. Twenty yards down the field we might get a wet hole and suddenly start sinking, and then you've got to use your brain. Things like that happen often. There's advanced systems they've come out with now. There's combines that have got GPS systems on them. The combine analyses the crop as it's combining. It'll tell you what the yield is for that crop on every single part of every field. It's taking in the crop at the front, it's telling you how much is there. It makes a map and the map is then fed into a computer. The computer sends the information to the sprayer or the fertilizer spreader so that the rates of fertilizer are changed according to the parts of the field that need more and aren't producing enough. OK, yes, that's brilliant technology. But how do you know the drill man hadn't just accidentally forgotten to do a little bit of the field and that's why the crop is thin? How do you know there wasn't an old house there years ago and that's a bit of stony land? There's so many different variants. It's all well and good that the computer thinks about the obvious. The sprayer will adjust its rates according to what the combine's information is. But it doesn't work like that. If you've got a wet hole because a drain is blocked in the field, you don't keep throwing fertilizer at it. You get out and sort the problem out. You've got to have the man on the scene.

The combines nowadays, the really posh ones, have cameras on the headers because the headers are so wide. They're thirty-five feet! That'll cut in one swipe. The man in the seat can hardly see out there. It's twenty feet each side, so he has a camera. The camera relays a message and that's what steers the combine for him. The same with the beet harvester. It's important to follow the rows of beet. Once the driver sits the machine in the row, it will carry on and drive and steer itself. It'll even crab-steer on the side to keep it so it's exactly right, to pick the beet up without damaging them. It's all maximizing as much as you possibly can, because there's no money to be made in cropping to start with, so you've got to make sure you've got everything good. The pass has got to be one pass made as good as possible.

The computer that goes with my other drill will tell me whether it's feeding the seed in correctly and even the amount it's putting into the land. The first time you'll know about the crop with this particular drill is when it starts to grow. If you've missed some bits then you'll know about it. We had a scenario: one of my two bosses was drilling the fields and after two weeks of drilling it started to come up. I saw the first field that came up and said to him, 'Do you have a problem with your drill?' A snail had crawled in the pipe and jammed it. He had drilled for two weeks with a dead snail jamming his seed, but his computer couldn't see the problem. Normally, you'd know about it because the seed would pour out somewhere else, but this drill splits into a Y in two places and the seed was running down at the same speed. It was just pouring more into the coulter next to it. He got the right amount of seed in the field, it's just that he had this little tiny row up the field. It needled him all year round.

So farming will never be completely computerized. There are variants and more variants. There are so many different soils right here.

I think I enjoy my drilling most. It's all pattern. Every time you roll a field, every time you loop round, there's a nice even flow and you get it all right, even and correct. Although it's a routine, it's just a once-a-year routine. It's not a production line where you put that bolt in there all day every day for six months. I suppose there's a routine; I turn round at the bottom of the field every time in a similar way. But, you know, I get out occasionally, see if I've got any seed. I deal with the weather, I improvise. You don't know what the soil will give you one day to the next.

Job satisfaction is the whole thing, when you can turn around and say, 'Cor, I did that.' And if there's a bendy line, then you'll know about that all winter. In the old days it used to be a real occasion and the weekends would be taken up with going round and looking at everybody else's work and seeing what Joe Bloggs across the hedge has been up to, seeing if he's as straight and as level as you are. If not they all meet down at the pub as a social event and take the mickey out of each other. I can take the mickey, but how far, how many miles, have we got to go to find some other farmer who even bothers, cares a damn, really?

*He teaches at Otley College, an agricultural college not far from Akenfield. Otley opened in 1974 and has grown from one lecturer, one barn and two tractors to its present 400 staff members and twelve-hectare site. The prospectus stresses the positive: 'Horticulture is the new rock 'n' roll,' it says under the heading 'Land-Based Studies'. 'Wherever you turn, gardening makeover programmes scream out of the TV. With an increase in profile comes an increase in jobs.'*

I remember *Akenfield* well – in fact I recently re-read it. It's very telling that Ronald Blythe began his book by describing the soils that the village is built on. The land, the soils, the topography, the geomorphology . . . if you're working within an agricultural area like Suffolk, working on the land day in and day out, you gain an understanding of the land. If you work in fields year in and year out, you learn about soils – which are the damp parts, which are the dry parts. You learn about the microclimates. You learn to instinctively know what will grow, what won't grow. Birdwatchers have a thing called 'jizz' – when they see, say, a little brown bird fly across their eyes, they can tell you what kind of bird it is; but when you ask them how they know, they can't tell you. That's what people who work on the land have. They have the land in their bones.

At Otley College, we started to see the number of folk interested in agriculture fall off in the 1980s. Through the late 1980s and early 1990s, agriculture declined even more and then came the build-up of other activities, from equine to landscaping. The trends were there for everyone to see. They were massively accelerated in agriculture because – crash, bang, wallop – we had BSE, quickly followed by foot-and-mouth.

Otley has its land-based roots and always will do. But because there are so few people coming into agricultural training now, it has diversified its course offerings: we do construction; we do equine; we do motor mechanics. We go right the way across the board. In order to stay alive we've had to diversify our student base; if we had stuck with our staples of agriculture, we wouldn't be here any more. Of those who are interested, quite often their fathers are farmers. There's generally a linkage. Very seldom would you find a youngster with no linkage to the land waking up and saying, 'Oh, I'd like to become a farmer.' There aren't the careers out there for those folk any more. In *Akenfield* there's a chapter where Blythe talks about people fleeing from the land and going into the towns. From 1967 to now, that process is complete. That's it – people work in the towns. Yeah, there are some folk who work the land, but they're sons or daughters of farmers who have already got the land. Or, alternatively, they are agricultural craftsmen who are working as contractors for themselves or the big estates. It's done. The process is a done job.

*Akenfield* reflected a typical Suffolk village at a time of massive change in agriculture. In the mid-nineteenth century, agriculture had gone into massive recession and didn't really climb out of it until the First and Second World Wars came along and everyone realized we were going to starve to death if we didn't do something. The government poured huge resources into agriculture, so that sort of thing never happened again. The Agriculture Act of 1947 geared everything to production, and that's what we see in *Akenfield* – production, production. It was only twenty-two years from the end of the Second World War. The people who fought in that war were in their late thirties, forties, and the whole mindset of that time was about insularity and about protecting your corner, making yourself secure. That is reflected largely in agriculture. We see a whole underclass of society shaking free of its fetters through transport and a better standard of living. We see the dreaded, but sometimes benevolent, tyranny of the landowners and farmers being broken. The youngsters were becoming more mobile and more able to express themselves because they had a few quid in their pockets. That all comes out in *Akenfield*.

Today, the government's priorities are all about managing the land, being guardians of the land, rather than agricultural production. Production is no longer the objective. We are now a European country; before we were a very insular country protecting ourselves – there was huge paranoia about what was happening in the countries behind the Iron Curtain and in the USSR. Now, that risk is lifted and people migrate across boundaries, economic migrants come over here and take advantage of the fact they can do casual labour on the land and then go back to their countries, where, with the exchange rates, if you're from the Baltic states, you go back from a season of picking and harvesting with a lot of money in your pockets. This has gathered pace over the last twenty years. You don't see the sort of typical, poorly skilled land worker you were still seeing in their forties in *Akenfield*. What you're seeing now are lots and lots of unskilled labour coming in from Europe to do those jobs. A few years ago I was sitting in my local pub singing Estonian folk songs to a guitar with all the Estonian fruit pickers who had come over for that. A lot of the agricultural workers who were tied to the land

and tied to the village are no longer tied to the village. They're off working in Ipswich or in other urban areas.

Big corporate farming of the 1960s to the 1980s made production the be-all and end-all. It treated the land as a series of inputs and outputs. So all the hedges were ripped out, the headlands were ploughed up. Everything was done to maximize production. In times gone by, that wasn't done; land wasn't just a unit of production. These days we're getting back to that ideal. We don't have to go in for mass agricultural production, in part because we can buy from Europe and the world for a bloody sight cheaper. From an ethical point of view, and from an air miles point of view, eating Kenyan sugar snap peas fills me with dread. It's awful. But it allows us to stop extracting as much from this land. We are now seeing a return to managing the land in a more biodiverse way. We have larger headlands. We have beetle banks that encourage predators to come in and knock out the pests rather than spraying them with phosphorus compounds every ten minutes. Also new technology like companion planting, things like that. These old wives' tales are turning out to be true.

As land has gone out of agricultural production, the pressure to build is increasing and increasing. They're not growing crops in this area, they're growing houses. Houses are the ultimate crop – the crop the landowner retires on, bless him. You can't help but notice the house prices here are completely ridiculous. We've been protecting our land for many years with Greenbelt legislation and the Town and Country Planning Act, but now we just haven't got anywhere to live, so we need another new wave of development.

In the 1960s, Akenfield was still quite a mysterious, closed community from an economic point of view. These days the villagers have a much more open approach to life. The majority of people living in the more salubrious houses in Akenfield either commute to London or Ipswich or 'tele-work' from home. This part of East Anglia is going to become the Surrey of the east. It's inevitable. We're already seeing an outbreak of 'horsyculture' all over the place. People with some money move out of London; they buy an old black barn, do it up, buy an acre and a half of paddock, put the horse fencing up, put the posting-rail fencing up around it, install a couple of horses . . . You see it breaking out all over the place.

How is the suburbanization of this part of Suffolk going to affect the psyche of the people working within it? There's almost a kind of apartheid system going on in some of the larger villages. The people growing up here now will be working for the rich. Infilling underneath them, you have the economic migrants coming over. Lovely old houses are owned by incomers who do the commuting and can afford to buy a Georgian house, while the descendants of the people who originally owned the houses are shunted off down to the council houses. I know it's a very simplistic overview, but that's how it is. A lot of the youngsters growing up in the bigger villages cannot afford to stay. That causes more of a fracture in the psyche of those people associated with the land. For the incomers, the increasing suburbanization is something they take as rote. A lot of the older folk who stay within the villages see it with horror. They're aghast at the whole thing. The old hearts of historic villages are becoming the playthings of the rich.

# PETER HOLLOWAY
## FARMER, 57

*He is a performer – the dramatic heart of the village. As a teenager his Christian rock band performed in a festival in one of Akenfield's pastures. They once shared a stage with Cliff Richard. He still plays saxophone and for years wrote the script for the annual Am Dram production while working in his fields. His most famous character is an exaggeration of a Suffolk Old Boy and he performs monologues at NFU events and local arts festivals, giving the audience a bit of 'hoomer'. 'You're a good ad-libber,' says one of the crowd after a show in nearby Saxmundham. Peter smiles: 'I just had libber for lunch.'*

I'm an import from Middlesex. My parents chose to move down here when I was about five or six, to a village near Akenfield, where I was brought up, and then we moved around a little bit. I always had a great interest in farming. My work was agricultural engineering and then . . . well, to cut a long story short, I became very friendly with a farmer's daughter, which I thought was a smart move. Ha ha. Her father was slightly disabled with hip problems, like most of the farmers had because of all the hard work they'd done over the years, hard jobs on the land: walking through with the horses, getting soaking wet and hefting hessian sacks and that sort of stuff. So he was finding it difficult and his son was too young to have much interest in the farming business at the time. However, I used to do a lot of work helping him. And then came the crunch time, when he was going to pack up and get out of farming, but then he thought that might be an opportunity to take me on and work alongside him. That would have been 1966 or '67. In that period I'd married his daughter and moved to Woodbridge. Because of the livestock they wanted someone on hand, so this particular house where I am, there used to be an outside herd running around here. I thought it would be a better idea to build a house here and move the stock, which we did. Because we had quite a few pigs. So just here, where this house stands, we had quite a few pigs right on this land. And so the house went up and then I moved from Woodbridge and I've been here ever since.

We farm for wheat, barley, beans and rape. That's our main cropping. And we also contract-farm, so in all with the contract-farming it's around 750 acres. We used to breed pigs, but breeding is very time-consuming. When you've got breeding stock on the farm you're always at work. If I step out here there's a job – either there's a water tank leaking, or there's a sow or something that's farrowing down that needs attention, or there's 100 weaners running around that have got out. I found that all a bit much.

So now we take pigs in at about twelve weeks old and fatten them under a contract, so they're just here with us during the fattening. The contract is with quite a large supplier of pigs, so they'll have people who breed the pigs for them in outside units. And then they take them at a young age into nursery units and then they'll come from the nursery units here to be fattened up, because we've got the existing buildings. We've got the straw, we've got the muck that goes back on the land, so it all works neatly around.

When we came into harvest this year the pigs all went from the unit, so we've had two months' break between batches to concentrate on the harvest and work from there. There's just my brother-in-law and I, we do most of the work. And for, say, harvest and some of the drillings, another brother-in-law who's a lecturer at Suffolk College. He has quite a long holiday and he comes and does the driving. He enjoys that. And then a local lad who will come and do a few hours in that peak time. Then it's back to just the two of us. It is a lot of work.

At the moment we can just about cope. It's nice to have people outside to call on if you do need a hand. I suppose that's what's killing farming: the profits aren't there to pay somebody full-time. One of the things, sadly, is the labour has to go. When I first came here there was about three or four. But then there was only 145 acres, you see. There wouldn't have been so many pigs . . . in my time, I'm talking about; previous to that a lot more.

The biggest change from then to now is that most of everything is planted for winter crops, which will be planted from mid-September to November. The actual genetics of the wheat have come on so much that they can withstand the winters. Back then they used to plant a lot more in the spring, so land would be ploughed with the horses and small tractors, then they would winter and that would make it good for, you know, going in in the spring and doing most of the plantings then. Now you've got machines, rotor-tillers, min-till machines with big horsepower which can actually break the land down with a few passes, where years ago that wouldn't have been possible hardly to get a good seed bed. Years ago they would have had to have relied on a good stiff winter to break the soil down to go in with the spring crops. The machines can do what the seasons used to do. Wheat and barley are strong enough to withstand the winter. Now you plant most of your crops before winter. And rape wasn't heard of before then. That wasn't, for whatever reason, a crop that was a big part of a farmer's rotation. It's what's called a good 'break crop'.

I think it's a great shame politics have interfered with one of the most important commodities of the country: providing food. What an important job that is. What can you do without food? The legislation and the difficulties that have been placed in our way ... take, for instance, apples. My wife works in schools. The government has come up with this idea to encourage youngsters to eat fruit in schools, which is fine. Where is all the fruit coming from? Portugal. Spain. And our local farmers are having to throw apples away. Our crops are exported mainly. We used to provide most of our own country with our own meat. Now the pig farmers have gone out of business. There's a big pig farm at the back here. He had 1,500 sows or more. That'd be several thousand pigs that would produce a year and he went out of business, mainly because of the imports. And that's just to name one because it's close.

I had some feed beans that went yesterday to Ipswich docks. There's a boat in there. It's a matter of taking what they're offering. A few years ago you could get 120 pounds for a ton. Today you get sixty. I know farmers do get subsidies, but without that we'd be completely out of it. But we don't want subsidies, we just want to farm our land. The chap who's growing the apples, he'd like to be selling those to the local school instead of letting them rot on the ground. I'd like to be selling my grain to local mills to feed local pigs who had local workers who fed the country. All sounds a bit fairy-like now, but that's how it is.

I've got two sons. One is a science teacher; the other works for a land agent, buying and selling land. One of them does help me a lot – but it's more from the armchair and computer side, rather than the hands-on side, which I enjoy. Go and get a proper job, I told them. It depends whether you like farming or not. As long as I've got health and strength and can get out there in the fresh air and do things I enjoy doing, that's important. You do see less and less opportunities for youngsters coming into farming, mainly because a lot of the farms are specialized and are operating with low labour. My sons can get better prospects doing other work than going into farming. I don't know who the farm will be passed to.

My sons are smart. They can start work at eight o'clock in the morning, have a company car, have six weeks' holiday a year. Get a bonus. Leave off at five o'clock in the nice environment. Who's the mug, really?

*The Kids*

## AARON 'HARRY' SEMMENCE and STUART CLARKE
## HORTICULTURE STUDENTS, BOTH 17

*They are doing a course in landscaping together, a one-year national certificate at Otley College. Today they will be studying plant identification. Later in the day it'll be tractor driving. Next year they'll do an advanced national certificate as an equivalent to A-levels. Harry's voice cracks slightly. Stuart has shiny blue eyes and is the shyer of the two. Their clothes are only lightly touched by current teen fashions. Harry keeps a photo of his refurbished tractor on his mobile phone.*

HARRY: I live just down the road in a little village. My grandad ran a butcher shop and slaughterhouse there. My dad's lived there all his life and I've lived there all *my* life. So we've been there for some time. I came here because I've always had an interest in the land, always loved the countryside – there's just something about the rolling fields. And nothing's the same: you can get up one day and see a tree and the next day it'll be different. There's all sorts of things living in it. I've never lived in a city, it's too busy. That busyness is coming out to the country. A lot of areas that were just open fields are being built up. It's kind of a worry to me that these houses are starting to pop up everywhere. I don't know how long it's going to be before more concrete is coming. You just think, Where's it all going to fit?

STUART: We've had to think about what we're going to be from a very young age. I've basically grown up with agriculture. I'm not going on to anything else. I can't do paperwork. I absolutely love this.

HARRY: I've got this tractor at home, a 1948 Grey Fergie. I saved up from working at the sawmill to buy it. It's been working in this area since it was new. It used to be just up the road, at Akenfield. On the log sheet it said it worked on the fruit farm there. I restored it all myself. I'm strange, I guess. I just thought, I've got to get a tractor!

It's an idiosyncratic old machine. It's got its own personality. Some days it decides it's not going to start. If I'm taking it to a show, it won't start because it doesn't want to go. And then you go in there the next day and it runs perfectly fine. It's got the rough old tin seat, so you get a bit of a numb backside after a while. I've driven new tractors and when you're in them you're encased in a little goldfish bowl. This one's nice because you've got the best air conditioning on the market and yet you can still hear all the birds sing. You hear everything around you. You can see things better. I feel connected because I get to see what's planted there. You watch the wheat, and even though it's not yours it almost feels like it's yours. You see it planted and watch it grow.

I've got to persuade Mum round before I get another tractor. It was difficult enough the first time. Her face when it arrived! She's come round to it, she won't admit it. It's at the bottom of the meadow. I've built a barn for it, so it's in there now, nice and dry.

STUART: I like looking after old machinery, restoring it. I do rotovators, strimmers, old Ransome mowers. I've got a really old mower, I think it's 1981. I picked it up at a car boot sale. I got the engine going again, painted it all up. I wouldn't sell none of my machinery. I just use it to keep myself happy.

HARRY: When I was at school it didn't seem like people were interested in the countryside. I worked for a few farms and saw some of them struggling on and on. I thought, I don't want to be like that. There's a lady in our village, she's got twelve cows and that's what she farms with. She's eighty-something and she struggles on using old equipment like her milking machine, one of those old hand ones, a portable, so you move it out from place to place. She milks by hand as well. Hers is a really old parlour and all the barns are dilapidated. Another farmer I worked for said it was an 'unsure climate'. 'It may not be such a good idea to go into it,' he said. At first they try to put you off with little hints. They complain about prices of wheat. After a while the hints get a bit bigger. One old boy said it wasn't worth going into it. His words were that he wouldn't let his children go into it. So I thought from then on maybe it was time for me to call it a day and do something else. I was thirteen.

We're both doing the landscaping course now, to learn how to landscape gardens in the countryside. As sad as it is, a lot of that work is going to come from new houses being built. In some ways they're helping but in other ways they're not. I think a lot of my working life will be on these new houses. There's a way of making it satisfying. If you do a good job that's the satisfying part. Seeing someone's face when you do their garden and they think, That's really good.

I take my inspiration from what's around me and from where the site is. I try to merge the garden in with the natural surroundings, so it won't stick out too much. Some gardens really stick out against the landscape. It's better to work with it. I'm learning about laying paths and trackways, treework. It's a broader thing than I expected it to be, but there are all these certificates. Like nowadays they want to make it so you can't even climb ladders. You've got to have a certificate to drive a tractor and diggers and things like that. Sometimes it's good to have, so you can show them you're trained. But it's a hassle sometimes.

The social scene is good here. Me and Stuart go up to a club called the Country Club on weekends, to play pool, have a drink and mix with people. Last week the Country Club was absolutely heaving. Loads of people up there – you could hardly move. They come from surrounding villages. I couldn't believe it when I got in there. The club was full, the deck was full, the dance room was full, and downstairs you had people playing snooker and pool. Girls come from surrounding villages, or they come to visit their friends who live in the village. You go up to town most of the time to see girls. I suppose that's what they did back thirty years ago. It hasn't changed that much.

We don't really talk to girls about all this. You keep your subjects separate; you just don't talk about the country. If we spoke to a girl about this kind of stuff, I think she'd run a mile half the time. You talk to girls about whatever you feel like – apart from tractors.

STUART: My girlfriend – we just got together not long ago – I knew most of her background. Her parents were in gardening. I just get on with them all so well. I talk to her about animals, gardens, and she loves it. It's just a matter of finding the right people to talk to.

If you're in the countryside, they need to be in the countryside. You know what you're talking about together. There's just a thing between you both which is really good. My girlfriend and I met through the college. She kept saying she wasn't interested and then all of a sudden we started getting on. By then I had passed my driving test. After that we went out. It was all good from there, really.

HARRY: If you start talking to them you can realize from body language and stuff what kind of person they're like and whether they'll run away or not. People who live in the town don't really understand it. They're nice enough girls, don't get me wrong, but if you spoke to them about farming or the land they would think it's all flat caps and neckerchiefs.

STUART: As for fun, I don't really watch movies. I like music, I listen to everything. Sometimes I listen to classical music, Radio Suffolk. Sometimes a bit of drum and bass.

HARRY: I listen to drum and bass most of the time. Fixing up a tractor goes faster when you're listening to drum and bass.

STUART: But in a garden you want something more relaxing. I'll listen to classical when I'm out there. One thing that's changed is that it's just shameful to see all that language die out, all the Suffolk ways. All the old sayings and that. You just don't hear none of them no more. 'Bit of an old hoo-ha.' I don't know why it's not being passed down.

HARRY: People come in from towns and mix in. It's near enough disappeared now. You don't hear any young people talking like it. People discourage them from talking like it because it's not proper.

STUART: You meet a proper Suffolk person, you laugh at their accent because it's so funny. Yet it's so pleasing to hear it. I definitely wish I had the accent. There's only about six people I know who have the accent. That's in a matter of hundreds of different people.

HARRY: There's a guy at the Suffolk Show who stands on a stand. You could pay him and he'd do a Suffolk yarn for you. He stood there. He was on show. He had such a rich accent that half the time you couldn't understand what he was saying. It was for a charity. He stood there and spoke. He had his big sideburns, typical of how you think an old boy would be – big old sideburns, hat and waistcoat.

We're pulling back towards Suffolk. You sort of realize what's being lost, I think. That's where farmers are going to make their money. Farm shops having exclusive meat from special breeds because people become more aware of their food, a lot of the supermarket stuff, they don't really know what is in it. My sister eats these Chicken Dipper things. I say to her, 'What's in that?' You look on the back and it's all E numbers.

STUART: It's really nice to just get your dog, go up the garden to the vegetable patch, get a carrot, take it down, wash it and start eating away at it. It's really good. Both my grandads used to do horticulture. My dad looks after forty-something acres of land which is all gardens. My grandad used to be on the garden side and maintenance side and my other grandad used to be a council worker for all the gardens. Now he's got an allotment. He used to go down there every day when he was young. Go down there, nick a few peas and carrots.

HARRY: I bought my tractor when I was thirteen, so I've had it a fair while now. It's still got some of the dents and battle scars from its working life; it's not immaculate by any means. I wondered if the old owners had any pictures of it at work, just out of interest. So I wrote to them ages ago, to the address that was on there: J. Youngman and Sons at Akenfield, the fruit farm. I didn't get anything back, so I just left it.

STUART: Seeing old tractors, it's great memories because you can just imagine what they've been through and the life they've had.

HARRY: I'll have to take my tractor up to see the old boys in

Akenfield. I'd love to see their faces when I take it to them. This one old boy who used to drive a tractor when he was younger, he had a tear in his eye when he got on it again. They get very attached to things. The day that tractor showed up on the farm for them – it must have been something.

I'm going to take it to some ploughing matches as well. They still do the ploughing matches – the farmers still compete to see who has the straightest furrows. I've got a plough for it, so hopefully I shall do that as well. You've got your markers and you basically line the centre of the bottom with the marker. Draw the first one out and work away from that first one. If the first one's not straight they're all not going to be straight.

My parents went out for the day so I thought it would be a good idea to plough up part of the field. My mother didn't say a lot when she came home. I don't think she was very impressed, but my furrows were all right. She wasn't worried about how straight my furrows were at the time.

*Shooting and Picking Up*

# ANDY YOUNGMAN
## FARMER, 45

*He is a handsome man with an occasional stern, appraising look. His family has owned land in Akenfield for generations. In the kitchen of his farmhouse, which stands at the end of a long drive, he taps a table with his fingers and creaks back in his chair. His overalls hang from the ceiling nearby, drying. Two of his children, a son and daughter, are talking loudly in the other room. They live in a nearby town with their mother; when he's with them, he takes them to their grass hockey games or out for lunch at the Three Horseshoes pub. When his daughter comes into the kitchen, she hugs his neck and leans into his shoulder.*

My family first came here in 1877. They were originally from Kent. They started off with Akenfield Hall; this house and the farm around here was bought at a later date, 1912. I went to school in Norfolk at a prep school, boarding school, and then at thirteen I went to the King's School, Ely, in Cambridgeshire. All my brothers and sisters went away to school as well. I used to spend a lot of time in the holidays cycling around the farm and seeing what was going on, helping if I could, or getting in the way. Later I worked on other farms and then spent six months in Australia before coming back here. My father died quite young; he was only sixty. I think that dropped me in the deep end, really. I was the one here, so I kind of took over. Things might have been different if he'd still been alive; I'd always thought of doing something else. But it's a beautiful place to live, and I enjoy the lifestyle and I enjoy the work. It's not as enjoyable as it used to be. The hours are much longer now at certain times of the year and there just isn't . . . there's very little in it now, so you're just working for nothing really. But I do feel a responsibility to the name. The Youngman name is known in this village. If you've been here this long and are lucky enough to take it over, then there's some sense of responsibility in carrying it on.

My father and uncle would have had a far different relationship with the men. When they were running the farm, they would go on tractors occasionally at lunch hours to relieve somebody, but you'd never see them on there all day. It was much more managerial in those days. They were authoritarian figures. My father and uncle were always around on the farm, going round and making sure all the jobs were done correctly and the way they wanted them done. If there were any problems they would go off and sort them out, get parts or whatever it was. There were a lot more men too. I'm a lot more hands-on than they used to be. I actually do a lot more of the work. We all sort of muck in together now, so it is quite different.

People that work on the farm are still paid an hourly rate. The pickers, the casual labour, is also done on an hourly rate. We used to do a lot of piecework, but when it became more important to have the quality at a much higher standard, piecework for picking apples was much more difficult. Obviously somebody working with piecework wants to pick as much as they can in the shortest time they can and make as much money as they can. That's when you get into problems with bruising and suchlike when you're picking apples. So we decided about ten years ago to go on an hourly rate. Don't think in the long run it's made too much of a difference, probably.

Normally I start at six. I go down to the yard at half-seven.

Depending on the time of year, I'll tell the guys what they should be doing. I may come back up here, have some work in the office. I may go to the workshop or I may be driving a tractor. I don't think I could do what I do without a mobile phone. There are people ringing up to deliver stuff, collecting loads of wheat and can they come that afternoon and can you load it? We used to have CBs in the tractor and didn't replace them. Now we've got the four mobile phones on a certain tariff, we get a lot of free minutes between us and it really doesn't cost us much. I think my grandfather would be depressed and amazed. I think he'd be depressed about the state of British agriculture for sure and the state . . . the decline of the numbers of fruit that we grow as well. I think he'd be quite sad about it. I think my father would too. He'd be pretty depressed at the state of British agriculture, much like a lot of the farmers in the UK. I think he'd be impressed by the technology that's come about. They'd probably be horrified by the size of tractors, thinking that they're too big. They might be right, because when the land's wet a big tractor does more damage to the soil structure. They would be thinking it's a disaster having a huge tractor on these farms, I would imagine. But we can't do without it any more.

My father would have known a very large percentage of the people who lived in the village, but I don't know that many now. There's very few people who work on the farm even during apple picking that live in the village. They're from surrounding villages, from Ipswich. I think we do put cards up in post offices to try and get people to ring up and we generally get enough for what we want. But some years it has been difficult. It's not great money. It's quite good money for picking apples, I think, but people want so much more out of life now, don't they? They're not prepared to get out of bed to go and pick apples for what they might consider to be a fairly low wage because it's only fractionally above the minimum. Why bother? Better off living off the state, or something. And it's not for a huge period of time, to be fair. A lot of people want something that's going to last for a long time if they're going to have a job.

We do get a lot of students who are going to do it before they go to university, which is great for them. But it's not like it used to be. I don't think you need to mourn it. It's just progress, isn't it? It's just life. I'm not sure everything that's progress is good, but it's inevitable, isn't it? Unemployment's much lower than it used to be. People are earning generally more money. Years ago for one of the men working on the farm to own a car was quite a big thing, whereas now everyone has a car. Mostly quite good cars. Many years ago, we had a proper store – two proper stores – that I remember and there were more before that. So you didn't need to go anywhere else. Now you can't avoid going somewhere else. The closest place you can go and do all your shopping is Wickham Market. It's only four and a half miles away but on your bike it was a bit of a trek if you had to come with loads of stuff.

I'm asset-rich, cash-poor. So I'm still rich in a sense but I can't get my hands on it, really. It can be frustrating. You still can't do a lot of things you'd like to do. You're just not making the money you feel you ought to be making because the value of your produce is much lower than you think it should be. My kids will not have the same education as I had. I can offer them a good education – they're educated through the state – but it's whether you think that private education is better than state education. I probably think it's not any more, though I feel they do have more opportunities to do things in the private sector, smaller class sizes and things like that. I seriously considered private education for my children but there's just no way I could have done it, not even for one of them, let alone three. Whereas you look back at the prosperity of the farm – it's no bigger than it was when my father and my uncle were running it. They educated nine children privately between them.

There isn't the cash available in farming to do that sort of thing now. I don't believe there is anyway. I've certainly thought about selling land. But the point about that is that if you sell assets, if you like, to privately educate your children, that's good for your children but it's not good for your business, because the asset you're selling is actually what you use to make your money, so the more land you sell the less money you can actually make from that business. So it's an ever-decreasing circle, really.

My life outside of farming is my children more than anything else. And I do shoot, I do enjoy my shooting. So that's something else I do during the winter. We've got various bits of wood here on the farm where you can shoot. I invite a few people around, old friends of mine who shoot, and they invite me to theirs. Or one or two of them go somewhere else and buy a day on someone else's farm. We may end up on someone else's farm they don't even know but they've actually paid for the day. I get invited as a guest. It's just the whole day. Great camaraderie. There's a lot of leg-pulling. It is a genuine, country day. It's us against nature to a certain extent. I don't know, I just really enjoy it. I enjoy being with people out there doing the same thing. On a lot of these shoots you have people beating, so people stand at the end of a wood and they'll walk through the wood and flush the birds out for the guns. It's all one – we still get involved with them as well. There's a lot of leg-pulling with the beaters. If there's a lot of people missing you'll get comments from them. I'm reasonably good. I'm an average to good shot.

My son Edward is quite keen on the farm but he just sees how difficult it is. He says, 'I can see it's a bit of a struggle sometimes. I want to earn more money than you do, Dad.' Fair enough. I think agriculture's going to change a lot in the next few years. A lot of these smaller farms will get swallowed up by the big ones. When that happens, if Edward was to take over this farm, I think he would then contract it out to someone else. He would hopefully keep the farm and have another job. You get an income from it, but not a sole income. You have to have side projects.

People think it's a lovely cushy life out here. Something that does frustrate me is when you get people complaining about the way farmers are, saying they should be restricted on what they can do, how they should plant hedges, plant more trees, or alter the size of a field. And yet you ask them, 'Do you like the countryside as it is now?' and they say, 'Oh yes, it's lovely.' Who made it like that? It's the farmers. The reason it's like that is because of farmers. It's not because of government. It's a shame. Most farmers are just like anybody else. They want to see a beautiful countryside. They're not out there to make a mess, to wreck it. They want to see it looking nice as well. Most of them have been here for years and years and they want a beautiful place to live. They're not going to make a hash of it if they can avoid it.

*Elegantly dressed in a cardigan, tie, pressed trousers and wellies, he stands in his small garage sorting apples. The air inside is thick with the smell of Coxes. Inside his house the walls are bare except for some small still-lifes. A stack of parsnips sits on his white table. A spray of dahlias shoots out from a glass of water. He speaks in a high, rhapsodic voice that chokes with emotion any time he has to consider the state of England today. We sit in his front room, on seats he keeps clean by covering them with single sheets of the* Daily Mail.

I came to a village just up the road from Akenfield when I was nine years old, in July 1923. It was a duke who owned the estate there and lived in the mansion. We moved into the cottage right opposite the main gates. Soon after we'd moved in, the duke moved to Scotland, the mansion was sold and they pulled it all down. Everything – all the lovely buildings, the house, the racing stables, it was all pulled down and goodbye to all that.

I'd been a nature boy. Very keen on birds, all sorts of birds. When I left school I worked on the estate there and they put me on to looking after all the poultry. The poultry man got axed, so they put me on to that. A boy of fifteen and I didn't know any of it. Later I worked on an estate where they would shoot thousands of partridges every year. All these birds flying up into the air and then coming back down. I learned how to pick up birds very well. When you're a picker-up you know how to watch the hit birds, the birds that are injured. The job is to pick them up after they've come down, to collect any bird that's injured. You don't want to pick up dead birds because anyone can pick up dead birds. There's no need to worry about them. You have to kill the injured birds to stop the suffering. To take care of a bird that was injured you'd just get hold of the head, give it a jerk and break its neck. Have you seen the Queen when she kills hers? She clouts them with a hammer, that's how she prefers to kill them.

There's no end of chaps today who have never had any experience with keeping. Even a lot of keepers today don't know about keeping. Some of them only ride about in a blooming truck and haven't the foggiest idea. You've got to learn all the different vermin, and how to catch them. Keepering isn't just looking after pheasants. There's 101 jobs to do. You've got to make places for them to bathe in, because they love dust-bathing just like a chicken does. You've got to look after food and all the various things connected to the vermin and that, because you've got rats and mice and stoats and hawks and owls and they're all totally different. You wouldn't catch a rat with whatever you'd catch a hawk with, would you?

Some of the gamekeepers these days have trouble finding a soft mouth. I've been annoyed with one of the local game-keepers these last couple of years. They send me some pheasants when they shoot. And not last year but the year before this keeper brought me two pheasants that were both bitten, one on the breast and the other all over the back. I said to him, 'Have you got a dog with a hard mouth?' That's what we call them when they bite like that. They shouldn't do it. You teach them not to. If they begin to maul a bird and push it about and shake it, then you take them and if you want to give them a tap you

give them a tap. We want the bird alive. We want it clean.
They're unsaleable when they're not.

When you're a picker-up, you've also got to clean up. You
make sure the ground you've covered is as clean as you can.
There might be two or three pickers-up. If you've got a bird you
can't find you can either ask one of them to help or tell them
you've got to stop a little longer to see if you can find the bird.
The object is not to leave any birds about. There are birds that
have been broken, and it's up to you to decide if they're fit to let
go or if you're going to kill them. It could be the littlest thing
goes wrong. There's a little bit wrong with one wing but that
needn't be very bad. Perhaps if it was left a few weeks it would
heal and that bird would be able to fly again. But for goodness'
sake don't let them go if they're going to die.

I don't go to the big shoots any more because I haven't got a
dog. Instead I go to some of the smaller shoots. The owners of
the estates say, 'Well, Freddie, you must come. Doesn't matter
about a dog.' These are the shoots I've been doing for years. I
got a lot of pleasure out of them because the guns who were
shooting seemed to get a lot of pleasure out of what I used to
do. I would come with Supersonic Jet. That was my dog's name.
I didn't name him; the chap I bought him off named him. He
was such a good dog – as good a dog as I've ever seen on a
shoot. I just lost him not so long ago. He was twelve and a half
and he was a cracker. A real cracker. A perfect dog to have on
estates like that. He knew everything you said and done to him.

I wear proper clothes to the shoots I go to now, because it's
right and proper to dress according to what you're doing, isn't it?
I dress in awful things when I'm cleaning pigs out and that sort
of thing, chucking muck about. I always dressed up when I
would go on my shoots. These gentlemen they all notice, you
see. I still got loads of ties: my sports ties, bowls clubs and
county ties. I don't have a lucky tie. I can tell you this: you don't

wear a bright tie on a shoot, just natural colours, if you like. You want to be unseen with the natural colours.

At the end of the shoot, for most of the gentlemen, the sooner they get on the better they like it. I wait for them. I see the guns and say to the gentlemen, 'Goodnight and thank you very much. I hope you had a nice day.'

Charlie, the head keeper, asked me to pick up for Prince Philip once. The head keeper has about five keepers on the estate. He called me one morning and said he wanted to see me, wanted to talk to me. So during the morning we got together and he said, 'We've got Prince Philip coming to shoot and I would like you to pick up for him. Will you?'

'Charlie,' I said, 'you know right well I'll do anything you want. You want me to, that's what I'm here for, that's what I'm paid for.'

He said, 'We shall most likely need a single picker-up to go with Prince Philip. I've noticed you know how to behave to these gentlemen. I've been watching things for a long while and I've noticed you're the best man about here, with a damn good dog. And you know how to behave.'

You see, I still touch my cap to all these gentlemen. It's been a habit all my life. My father taught me to do that. Even though I was a little boy, when the owner of the estate came down from London, my dad used to get me to say, 'Morning, sir.' It's such a habit that I do it nearly completely now. Like I said, in the garden or in your dealings with people or anywhere else, you want to make habits of the good things of life. Doesn't matter about the bad things, you can let them float. But all the good things in life, try. Always touch your cap. 'Morning, sir.' And whether you take it off or leave it on it doesn't matter, providing you get hold of it and drop your head a bit.

I got on wonderfully well with the gentlemen. I don't remember having a bad word in the fifty or sixty years I was down at the estate. I try in life to please everybody I get in contact with.

When I was picking up, gentlemen would come from all over the place. I couldn't say exactly where – I just knew them as Lord So-and-So or whatever. I'd be introduced to them before they started in the morning. I say this because so many people talk of gentlemen as if they're buggers. They're not. I don't remember a gentleman I disliked in any way. Gentlemen have not changed too much over the years. Some of the younger gentlemen are a little more talkative than the older gentlemen. But in all due respect to any of them, they know behaviour and that's a lot.

About four years ago there was a shoot down in Hoo, near the church. One of the guns hadn't arrived and we all stood waiting out in the yard and presently this vehicle pulled up. He was a bit late. They opened the door when the gentleman hopped out and we all stood around waiting for him, really. He just stood there looking across towards us and before he got his gun out he came straight across to me because I'd seen him before.

I said, 'Morning, My Lord.'

He looked at me in the eye and said, 'That's enough of that, Freddie. It's Eric to you.'

That's what he said to me. Now, is there anything wrong with that? It's his way of teaching me how to talk to him. He don't want me to say 'My Lord' every day. He wants his Christian name. That's his orders. Mind you, I'm proud of being able to say to him, 'Morning, Eric,' after I said, 'My Lord.' That, to me, is a gentleman. He's not very old, but a proper little man to be with. During the day it's Eric. I don't 'My Lord' him till he go home at night. When night comes and we're going to part, I'm Freddie, just the same, but he's My Lord again.

See, we're not all the same, are we? I mean, I have met some people and been totally different than I have with others. I have had a wonderful life. I've been proud. That's been my side of the pleasure for myself. Other people have had the pleasure out of shooting. I've picked up. I got on so well with the owner and his son. When I left they gave me a silver ashtray for picking up for forty years. It's silver. Made in London. And it's mine. There's hundreds of people who do it for as long as that. They don't get the same treatment.

When I was picking up for Prince Philip I was with him all day. At the finish of the drive it was no good for me to say, 'Bugger it, I'm going.' I waited for him to go connect with the other guns. See, you have to make sure you don't run home all in a hurry. I waited till he was a little bit unruffled and then I went and said, 'Excuse me, Your Highness. Goodnight and thank you very much.' And I tipped my hat.

*Farming III: 'All the Glamour and the I.T.'*

# JONATHAN PIRKIS
## FARMER, 57

*In 1957 his father bought a 300-acre livestock farm in Akenfield for 50 pounds an acre. He now runs the farm and has added to it gradually – a little at 1,400 pounds an acre and more at 3,500 pounds an acre. He has the reddened skin of a man who has spent his life outside. He couldn't look more like an Englishman, he says. 'Generally my wife gives me a little criticism for wearing check shirts and looking very much the part of the farmer.' He's got an oiled linen waistcoat with plenty of pockets. He describes himself as a farmer except when he is speaking to the bank manager. Then he becomes a farmer/land owner: 'It elevates me a little.' It is just after lunch and he is clearing the remains of fresh vegetables from the table.*

Father was in the army during the Second World War. He went to the desert, was captured, spent time in a prison camp in Tunisia. He had had the option of staying on the farm, but all his mates went to war so he went to war. In my father's day, anybody who was anybody reckoned they ought to go off and do their bit. Nowadays, it always seems to be somebody else's war. At the end of it, there were a lot of people coming back who had seen the results of people not having enough to eat. I remember my father telling a story of a Russian prisoner-of-war

camp next to the English one. The Germans had complete con-
tempt for the Russians because they felt they wouldn't have any
retribution from them, whereas they were a little more careful
with us because they weren't quite as confident. The Germans
put a dog into the Russian camp to quell a riot that was going
on. Within about half an hour the Russians had skinned the
dog, eaten the flesh and hung the skin up on the wire. You
come away from those experiences knowing the effect of hunger
on people. I can remember ration books, a little blue book, and
you had so much orange juice, so much butter and so much
bacon. I certainly never went hungry, but I just felt that food
was important.

School didn't do anything for me. My parents had a friend
whose son had gone to a sea training school – the HMS
*Worcester* on the Thames – and it seemed like a good idea. We'd
been brought up with visits to navy ships. They'd come in to
Harwich and Father would take us down to see them, so I think
the idea of going into the Merchant Navy appealed because it
had this feel of commerce and this great idea of carrying things
from A to B, from where it was to places of shortage. I spent
three years at the HMS *Worcester* and came out as a cadet on a
merchant ship. For about ten years we did runs to Barbados,
Trinidad, Guyana, Venezuela, Colombia, and all around the
southern United States. We'd come back having unloaded in the
Grenadines, then load up with sugar in British Honduras. This
was 1965 through to 1976, so I saw a changing world.

Life on the sea was exciting, and the worse the ship, the hap-
pier the crew. We sailed on a ship with a triple expansion engine
and a little turbine stuck on the end to get the last few pounds
of steam out. It was hot; the steam made it hotter. There was no
air conditioning but the atmosphere was wonderful, probably
due to the amount of beer. The modern bulk carrier has air conditioning, so you don't tend to sit outside. You sit in the cabin
and read a book. On these journeys we would sit under an

awning with the smell of a barbecue coming from down on the afterdeck. It was a great feeling of mateyness.

The ship was usually filled with Liverpool lads or Scottish lads. They were fairly townie-orientated. I think they thought I was a bit of an outsider because I didn't have a Liverpool accent. But they were great mates. We used to go ashore together and played lots of cards. They were into their football and I don't think they really had much interest in Suffolk. I'd get nick-named Captain Birds Eye because of the peas, they'd seen that on the telly. I suppose at that age I was going out away from Suffolk and I was tending to forget it. There was this great feeling of going out and seeing places that were there to be seen.

Then, when I was nearly thirty, I'd had enough of it. I think it was the animals I thought of most. The dogs and cats. I remember books like *Watership Down*, which was very English, and even Jane Austen. I remember having a vivid dream. The ship was working twenty-four hours a day in Kenya, so we would work twelve on and twelve off. I did the nights and then went ashore to a rather mosquito-ey hotel and tried to get some sleep, though in that sort of heat it was hard. I don't know what it was, but I had the most vivid, colourful dreams I've ever had of Suffolk, of the countryside. It was all in great contrast to the heat and the sea and the beach in Kenya. The dream consisted of these wonderful lush green fields and hedgerows, a typical English, Suffolk spring. So in the subconscious I was obviously feeling a longing for it. I suppose it's always a natural tendency to remember the best parts of things. Hence the spring – I didn't dream of the bleak winter, snow and black hedges. Now that I'm here I tend to read books about the sea.

My father was nearly seventy when I came back here. I never had a good relationship with him. I remember bringing something like 70,000 tons of wheat back in one ship from California, through the Panama Canal and off to Russia. Father was sucking his teeth a bit because this was all coming to take over his market. I see parents nowadays rushing off to watch their children playing rugby and all that sort of thing. There was none of that with my parents. I think it made it easier to just get on with the job. He happened to have the farm, which I wanted, but I wanted to do it the way I wanted to do it and not the way he had done it.

I went to Writtle Agricultural College in Essex for a mature students' course, and then I came back to help my father. I was prepared to put up with what it took to get in this position. I bought out my brothers and ended up with a mortgage and the rest. I bought about 30 per cent more land because I wanted to have enough to justify employing a man; now I can't justify one man on this size of business.

On this farm now we tend to grow things like milling wheat for bread. We have a contract with a company up in Manchester for this special variety called Arrowwood, and that gets taken right up there because they want this particular variety and they'll pay for it. We grow the peas for Unilever, Birds Eye. They're quite a good profitable crop most years, not always. We tend to go for slightly upmarket things we can grow on this soil, and if I can get that harvest in time we get a better price for it because the weather hasn't got at it.

Of all the places I went to, I never saw anything like Suffolk. To go up Highgate Lane on a slightly murky evening and see those mauves and greens and the colours of the trees and the way they follow the ditch-lines and hedge-lines – it's just unbelievably beautiful to me. I didn't see anything approaching it on my travels because in most of the countries I've been to the landscapes are so much bigger. You don't have the subtlety of variations, all these variations over a small distance. I remember a neighbouring farmer who took a train across the United States. He said it just doesn't change for hour after hour after hour and then the next day it doesn't change either. Whereas here you go ten miles up the road and you're in something completely different. Even the land on the other side of the A12, because it's light soil, is different and quite markedly so.

The A12 seems to be the demarcation line, I suppose because it's near the River Deben. It's more salty and sandy and flatter, whereas up here it's heavy clay soil, more difficult to work and rather horrible when it gets wet. We tend to grow things like wheat, oilseed rape and peas, whereas on the lighter soil they're much more diverse. They can grow veg crops and I suppose the latest thing is this grass for turf, great swaths of green, very flat grassland, which you could never do on this soil. You could never get it up.

You spend so much time with the land you get to know it very well. You get to know your machines. I suppose nowadays this idea of changing machinery puts an end to that, but I can get quite fond of pieces of equipment I've used. Autumn time is my favourite part of the year, because the colours are so diverse: the variations, the subtleties. It's a time of great promise. You're forward-looking, putting these seeds in the ground in the hope things are going to go forward and it will be productive, whereas harvest is the day of reckoning. It's either there or not.

I think my wife gets a bit fed up sometimes when I get my farmer face on. There are times when the devil drives you. That's partly what makes me do it. The idea of going out at seven in the evening to go finish a rape crop, going till after midnight. It's quite an exciting thing to be involved with.

What's driven me for the last twenty years is seeing starvation in Africa and Honduras and other places I stopped. It puts food in a different context. The idea of the supermarket with shelves stuffed with food and obesity being a big problem, you know, it does affect me. I still feel food production is important because no one knows what is around the corner. Local food production rather than global production is a very important idea because of fuel shortages, strikes, conflict. Also, you can monitor what goes into it and how it's done and all that sort of thing, whereas if it's produced in South America we don't know what's gone into it.

The great difference between Akenfield a generation ago and now is that even on a small farm then you had three or four men; now there's only one. I can give him jobs like painting fuel tanks, but he's not going to want to be here in the winter with very little to do when it's all a bit cold. If you've got a very young chap you really have to be there with him, but I can't do that because I've got paperwork and meetings. You have to keep them interested. It would be great if we had something like turkeys or Christmas trees or some other small crop, but there's enough people doing that as it is. I've thought of things for the winter months but nothing new. On a small scale I had visions of growing really hot peppers, but there just isn't the market for them. People like the conventional peppers; they don't really go for the hot. Even our taste is a little bit staid in Suffolk.

It comes down to this labour business. There are so many houses being built, so many roads, that the building trade is taking all the manual labour. The money is there and certainly among the younger ones they just think, Well, why work on a farm when I can get twice as much building a road?

The chap I had for the last four years left last autumn to go into the building trade. He was a plasterer and could get twice as much as I could offer. He was going to go in the building trade in the winter and early summer and come back and help me in the autumn, and he rang up one night and said, 'I've got this contract that's going to go all throughout the autumn.' That was that. I think he wanted a bit of a heart-to-heart on the phone but I wasn't really feeling inclined to give him one. I wished him the best of luck.

In the future, there is a possibility that the big farmers will have labour problems, they'll have machinery problems, they'll have logistics problems and if it gets much tighter they just won't do it and farms will be split up and small people may come back in again. It's a possibility. Large-scale farming has never worked over here because we've got small fields and high population. And it doesn't seem to me the large-scale farmers are making big profits. They never look very happy to me.

But I think the biggest thing against English farming carrying on in any great way will be just human interest. The average school kid isn't really interested. They don't want to be on their own, they don't want to be in the mud and wet. I'd be happy if my own son was interested. But I think I'd rather he went away and did something else first. When I see young people going straight into the farming business, by the time they're forty they're wondering whether they did the right thing. Whereas coming into it a bit late, like I have, and seeing what the alternatives are, it keeps you going through the downsides.

If I were really trying to be optimistic, I would just hope that some kids will see through all the glamour and the I.T. and the form filling and the computer screens and want something real. That's my big optimistic hope: that consumerism will seem so shallow that they'll want to get back to reality and get into producing something that we can touch and that we all need.

*He is a pig farmer by trade and used to run a company that spit-roasted hogs at social events. He has a thick thatch of hair and a confident way of speaking that comes from putting forward farmers' arguments for years.*

I'm the fifth generation on our little 200-acre family farm. My father wanted his children to have a good enough education so we wouldn't have to farm if we didn't want to. That worked well with my brother and two sisters; it didn't work for me. I quite like the farming side of things. I went to college, left college, fell in love with skiing, went abroad, kept pigs in Switzerland and Germany. The only thing I knew how to do was to look after pigs – that was my skill – and I wanted to ski, so I put the two together after a couple of years.

In Switzerland we worked six to six, six days a week, six to nine on Sundays. We used to ski in the evenings. There was a floodlit slope in town, so at seven I'd jump in the car and head off. You could ski up to the bar and drink with your skis on and then head off again. It was good for a couple of years. Eventually I came home, set my own pig herd up and after a while merged that with the family pig herd. I took over the management of the family farm. I also started rowing at the local rowing club at around the same time and one day they said, 'Chris, could you do a barbie for 100 people?' I thought, Ah, I'll cook a pig. I trotted down to the farm workshop and built my first spit, which was hopeless actually, but it was a start. Everyone eating the pig said, 'This is fantastic,' so I diversified into hog roasts. I cooked pigs at events. I started a catering business and built it up. I was roasting for twelve years as well as running the farm.

We were called Hoggies. We built some fancy kits. There was an electric motor turning the spits, lights in there so you could carve at night. It's not always easy getting a pig on to a spit. You have to get the pig to run at you very fast to skewer itself . . . No, not really. But you do learn some tricks on how to get it into position – the key bones. You're collecting the pig from the abattoir so all the guts are out of it. You just push the skewer up the back end. There are clamps you slide on inside the belly. Keep pushing the shaft through and out of the mouth and then hammer the clamps back. The most effective form of keeping the whole thing together was to use chicken netting. We started with charcoal but moved to gas to get a nice brown crunchy crackling and succulent meat inside. Pigs are designed for roasting, they really are, because all the fat is right underneath the skin. The ideal is a pig with a half-inch of fat, cooked for six or seven hours really slowly.

The Meat and Livestock Commission were promoting meat at the time. I went along to them and said, 'Look, everybody's raving about Hoggies. Are you going to help me promote this?' They said, 'No, quite the opposite. We want you to stop, because we've spent twenty years trying to get butchers to take carcasses out of windows and put out diced meat. We don't want the public to connect the animal with the meat. Here you are roasting what is obviously a whole animal. We want you to stop.' And I thought, I'm not going to stop. The public aren't that daft. We used to cook the pigs with heads on and occasionally you'd get a squiggy girl who would say, 'Ooh, I don't like the look of that.' But as a farmer I'm keen for people to know that when you eat pork it comes from a pig.

I did that for twelve years. Then, with a young family, I thought, I can't do this the rest of my life. So I sold it lock, stock and barrel in 1997.

It's a culture, farming. Farmers tend to have grown up in farmers' families and that's why they're farming. If you're cruel you say they're there by accident of birth. If you're kind you say it's a really enjoyable lifestyle growing up on a farm. The reality is that when that character looks at what he's good at, there might be other things he can do (or she can do – a lot of ladies in farming, don't forget the ladies); but if you enjoy what you grow up with, you're very reluctant to let go of it.

The average age of a farmer in the UK is sixty. The average age of a livestock farmer is sixty-eight. So structural change is going to happen very soon, purely because of the age of the farming population. Out of the 50,000 national workforce about a tenth is in this eastern region. We've added it up. There are 8,000 active farming businesses in the region. They don't own the land, they're actually doing work on other people's farms. There are about 15,000 people holding land in the region. On average you've got one farmer who's looking after somebody else's patch of ground. Now, as those older farmers go on and retire or move on to semi-retirement, they're just going to keep asking their neighbours to run that patch of ground for them. So you're going to see more and more opportunity for someone who dearly wants to farm. He's going to be offered and he's going to have opportunities to take on more land, so the people who psychologically can't do anything else, the ones who can't think of anything else other than farming, they'll be able to farm bigger acreages and expand.

The limit only comes with the size of the machinery and getting the machinery into the fields and in between fields. You get a machine more than four metres wide and it would be hard to move down Suffolk lanes. Right now we're starting to see the limit in those six-row sugar beet harvesters. These are big combines. A couple of years ago I was going down one of the small lanes near home. I have a neighbour who farms 2,000 acres. He's got a combine that he was moving around to where he was going to start cutting. He came up the road with these huge flotation tyres. They were on the verge, so there was actually nothing of the combine touching the tarmac of the road. The thing was so wide he was just running on the two verges. There were quite steep banks either side; he was way up there. I could have sat my car in the middle of the road and he would have driven right over the top of me. They are enormous machines but they can't keep getting larger in this country, purely for the physical aspect of moving them between fields.

You look at farmers and farm workers these days and they stand side by side. You would think they were partners in the firm rather than employer/employee. It's much more of a blurred distinction between the two. They're friends. I see that across the board these days. Farmers are desperate to keep good guys. I talk to farmers in the outdoor pig industry and ask them if they want to train their guy up. 'No, I don't want to train my guy up. He'll get poached. I'm going to look after him. I'm going to be really friendly and make the job so enjoyable that he doesn't want to move anywhere else, because poaching happens. A neighbour or someone five miles down the road comes along and says, "All right, I'll pay you another couple of grand a year, do you want to come and work for me?"'

That's why the image of the old landowner with his stick and the poor hungry serf of a farm worker is so historical and so out of date. Public perception is that the farmer is a landed gentleman who never gets his hands dirty and instructs his man to do his work. The reality is that because the money's gone the farmer now sits in the tractor seat and gets his hands dirty as well as getting in the farm office and doing all the paperwork. We started training programmes four years ago. When we started farmers were happy to turn out in the evening to do a computer course. Now they say, 'Don't put it on in the evening. I've spent all day on the tractor. I'll come along to your thing in the evening and fall asleep. Put it on in the afternoon and that makes me get off my tractor, when I can still concentrate.' So just in the last four years they're saying, 'Look, we're so damn busy we're sitting on tractor seats far more than we ever were.' Six o'clock at night and these sixty-year-old guys are whacked. But for the first twenty, thirty years of their life they weren't working so hard. Now that they're sixty they're working harder than they've ever done.

Farmers don't traditionally retire. They die with their boots on. One of the hopes of this new subsidy system is that these sixty-year-old farmers won't be compelled to work harder and harder in order to produce an income. When the subsidies arrive it means they're going to be paid next year to be a custodian of the countryside; their mentality should be, OK, I know that cheque is going to arrive for me doing a responsible job with this patch of ground. I'm then not going to work so hard at producing bumper crops the whole time round. I'll still keep cropping, but it's not so important now because I know whatever I do with those crops this subsidy cheque will arrive for me being a responsible citizen looking after this patch of ground for the country.

There is a big sea change going on at the moment. My hope is that it will enable the seventy-year-old farmer to say, 'I'm going to get that cheque so that young lad over there – he might be thirty years old – that young lad on the neighbouring farm, it would really help him to run his operation over a bigger acreage. I'm going to offer him my acreage, I'm going to offer him my farm to work, no cost. He can come in and crop it. If he makes a profit good on him, but I just want to see it looked after.'

What's most frustrating about being a farmer is that you have to stick to a set of rules, but then the public turn round and blame farmers for sticking to them! In the 1960s and 1970s, the government policy was to take out hedges and increase the size of fields. So farmers went and did that. Ten years later, everyone asked why they did it. All those nice hedges for wildlife and conservation and so forth. Well, it was done because after the war this country was convinced it had to increase the efficiency of farming, so it could feed itself. The Agriculture Act of 1947 said we will increase our self-sufficiency in food and this is how we're going to do it: we'll take some hedges out and we'll drain the land so it grows more and you can use bigger machines on it. That worked, there's no doubt about it. By the late 1970s we were as self-sufficient as we possibly could be. We were growing 75 per cent of the stuff in the shops.

Now, because of the environmental agenda, the self-sufficiency level has dropped back to 65 per cent. Food can be produced cheaper elsewhere in the world. Eastern Europe, South America, Australia can produce cheaper grub. There's a lower cost of production and it's being shipped in because the cost of transport is relatively low.

For older farmers it was a huge change to be suddenly asked to produce less, to grass things down. The countryside is for wildlife conservation, they were told, the whole farming operation should become less intensive. Whereas for fifty years they'd been told to become more intensive, to grow more, now we're saying no, don't want that any more, and half of that is because we're now an affluent country. We can afford to not grow wall-to-wall wheat. We can afford to take a more benign attitude to where our food comes from. If it's cheaper to bring pork in from Hungary, we'll bring it in from Hungary rather than have our own pig farms. And that argument runs until for some reason we can't ship it in. If the Channel Tunnel gets blocked or the transport costs go sky high, then this country will start to look pretty silly, because we've ignored food security. I think every nation should be able to produce half and preferably two-thirds of what it needs.

I don't think we should go back to growing everything ourselves, but we shouldn't dumb our agriculture down so we're only producing, say, 10 or 20 per cent of what we need, and we have all these pretty flower meadows people can walk in, and everyone says, 'Oh, isn't the countryside beautiful, isn't it wonderful?' Farmers just become park keepers. It's like pressing a self-destruct button, isn't it?

European workers started arriving here quite recently, about five years ago. As soon as they worked out the timetable of the accession countries to come into the EU, the tap was turned on. It's relatively straightforward for them to move over here and earn big money, as far as they are concerned.

They have a very strong work ethic, so they've been a joy to employ. It's the professionals and middle class from the ten accession countries who have come over here so far. Farmers will tell you it's accountants, doctors, dentists that they're employing. The prime reason for them coming over is that they want to build their house. In six months a couple can come to this country, work like stink and earn enough to go back and build themselves a house. If you're a young professional couple, you've just got qualified, you say to yourself, 'We'll take six months out before we're locked into a job and we've got kids and so forth. We're going to trot off to the UK and do a menial, manual job – but we're doing it for a real reason.' So they're intelligent, they've normally got a good grasp of English and they've been great to employ.

Anybody who wants to work on a farm only has to make a

dozen phone calls and they've got themselves a job. Organic farmers who need a manual labour force to do some hand-weeding couldn't get English people to do the job. You've got this whole culture that's still in their twenties or thirties who think that manual labour is too hard, too difficult. They've been sold this office job. They sit in front of the computer and don't have to work too hard to get their money. You put them in a field and say, 'Right, here's twenty acres of carrots – pull all these weeds out of it.' They think, Bloody hell, I don't like that idea! They tend to turn up for a day and then you don't see them again, whereas the people from Eastern Europe haven't been sold that cushier lifestyle, so they're quite prepared to get down on their hands and knees and weed a whole field.

The prediction is that in three years' time we'll be farming 25 per cent of what we are now. Five years after that it's going to halve again. You've got to say to yourself, 'What am I going to do? Am I just going to sit here and look at incomes dropping? If the world wheat price goes sky high it's not going to be an issue, but that probably won't happen.' So I took myself off to college to get an up-to-date degree in agriculture with a lot of marketing and management mixed in. I was forty.

I went to work for the East of England Development Agency and the ADER project. That stands for Agricultural Development in the Eastern Region. The whole idea is making farmers aware of the world they're living in now and where it's going to move to. Spread your risks, start to rely on more than crops and animals. Start to look at other enterprises, start to think about it because over the next three years you've got to have done something. The subsidy cheques will dwindle. The money's not going to drop that much for three years but after that it's really going to start to be cut back. The East of England Development Agency does not want thousands of farmers going bankrupt. What they want is a vibrant rural economy that helps the region's economy. If every farmer starts up another little business, if every farmer is taking extra income from somewhere else, then he will be staying in the village, he'll keep farming the land.

You'd be surprised at what these second jobs could be. There's the pig farmer who became a comedian. And so he either comes up and does his stand-up routine himself or he's also a partner in a double act. He's got this gift. He used to keep people amused down at the pub. I've heard him once. You tend to cringe a bit at some of his jokes, but then comedy's always a matter of taste, isn't it?

## LUIS MARQUES
## MIGRANT FARM WORKER, 42

*He is one of the directors of Meta, an organization that helps migrant workers in England. 'I can't walk down the street. It should be a five-minute walk to the office. I can't do it in five minutes — I get stopped too much by people asking for my help. A lot of people come asking me to fill documents out for them or go to the bank with them. I remember the advertisements. In Portugal they come in the tabloid newspaper. They're not large advertisements but these agencies promise large. Better life. A much better existence in the UK. Then you arrive and find out there is no agency. You have to pay 250 pounds to the man who picks you up at the airport. It only gets worse from there.'*

I came over here three years ago. In Portugal if you are more than thirty-five you are very old to have at work. I don't understand why. I had positions in marketing and management. I had my own company working with the government. I sold medical equipment. Ninety per cent of the market for incubators for the babies was mine. I sold computerized scanning machines. From needles to scanning machines, beds, anything. If they needed, I could keep an entire hospital working with my equipment. It didn't work out. From the factories where I bought the equipment I had to pay in thirty, thirty-five days. After the payment they would send me the equipment. After that I put the equipment in the hospitals, health centres, and I'm waiting one year, two years before I receive the money. As I didn't have the financial structure behind me it's impossible to go into business.

I have a good CV for the positions in Portugal but they can't accept me. I'm over-qualified. I told them, 'I only need the job.' Excuses they gave! I met a Portuguese man from England – on holidays he came back to Portugal. He told me you have to come with me to England because here you don't have any kind of chances and I can help you in England. So I made a decision to come to England. I came to his home. He was my employer. I came to his home and so this moment he is in Portugal and I am still here.

I have my son in Portugal. He's twelve. 'Father has to work,' I said to my son. 'Here in Portugal Father has no work so I have to go abroad.' Of course it was very difficult. It's very difficult for him and for me. We phone every day. At weekends we spend a lot of hours on the Internet together. Sometimes we chat online, we talk with the microphone, or just with the Messenger. It's very difficult. We are divorced, my son's mother and I, but we have a good relationship. He tells me what's happening in school, what's happening on the weekend.

When I came to England I started working in a condom factory in Cambridge, but then the factory moved to India and closed the doors. Everyone was fired. The owner of the factory was SSL International, the owners of the Durex. I moved on. The first farm I worked at I worked on the line. Every kind of flowers was being grown on the farm – the flowers came down the line and you have to cut the weeds, put the labels on. Cut the weeds, put the labels on . . . It's like a factory, a line. I don't know too much about flowers, but I could cut the weeds and put the labels on. It was my first time on a farm. I didn't get any training. They only told me you had to do this, this and this. Cut weeds, put this label on this one. When you've finished this you go there and do the same, but with different labels. In the line they put the pots with the plants and the different labels near the pots. I just put on labels. Labels, labels, labels.

Most of the people came from different countries. There is English, of course, but most of the people who work in that farm were from different countries: Israel, Spain, one or two French, and most of them from Portugal. We came to survive. We have to do everything that appears in front of us. If we can earn money we have to do the job. That's the reason you can see so many Portuguese in the field and in so many factories.

I worked at another farm near Bury St Edmunds. The owner worked together with us. I worked not on a line but right in the ground, in the field. I pick up the flowers, I put weedkiller in the fields. Basically at that farm it was trees and plants for gardens. A lot of people went to the farm and went around the fields – 'I want this one, that one,' they would say. I would have to pick up. Eight hours a day. If it's raining, the owner didn't want us outside. So we went to the warehouse and worked there. We worked on the orders, joining the plants with an order. We'd sort them. There were seven or eight people there. That work is like family work. The owner works with us. It's a good environment. The pay, I think, was five pounds an hour.

I never had any experience on a farm before. My experience is numbers. But it was good experience, I liked it. I was the only Portuguese at the second place I worked. They received me very well. They helped me when I sometimes didn't know what to do. We stood together out in the trees. There were only seven or eight working there. In the first farm there were fifty people. It's completely different. I never had any kind of problem. But then, I speak English. The big problem is communication, not racism. Communication between the Portuguese and the English, or between the Polish and the English, because the level of education of the Portuguese people who live here is very low. Sometimes they don't read or write even in Portuguese, so it's very hard for them to learn another language when they don't even know their own. It's very hard. To solve this communication problem is not in one year, two years, three years. It will be solved probably by the next generation, or two generations ahead.

*His voice is warm and not heavily accented. He is passionate on*
*the subject of agriculture and even more passionate when it*
*comes to agriculture in Poland. He is rushed: his plane back to*
*Poland leaves from Gatwick later in the day.*

Kowalski is like Smith in your country, it's a very common
name. There are many of us. I come from the southern part of
Poland. I grew up in a small town of about 10,000 people called
Tarnawa, which is about one hour from Kraków. My grandfather had a small farm, nothing like what you'd get here. My
mother worked in a milk processing plant and my father
worked part-time on the farm and in transport the rest of the
time.

The first time I came over here to work was 1998. I was
studying agriculture and economics in Poland. It was my
second year and I had done a placement for economics, now I
was to work in agriculture for a while. I was brought over by an
organization called Concordia, which brings students to the
farms, and I started in May at a farm that had strawberries and
apples. After two weeks of picking fruit I was given more jobs to
do. My driving skills and supervisor skills were put to use. After
one month I was driving the minibus and the forklift. It was a

medium-sized farm. There was all kinds of work: irrigation and organizing the workers. We came from all over. There were people from Poland, Bulgaria, the Ukraine, Belarus, Macedonia and even Hungary.

Most of the Polish people who have not been abroad before come by coach, so they can see the other countries on the way. They've never seen Germany before or Belgium. From Poznan the coach ride takes seventeen hours. From the eastern side of the country it could take twenty-four or twenty-six hours. I think for people coming for the first time, it can be lonely. I was going alone the first time, but most people go with someone else. It wasn't so easy the first time, but my motivation was high.

The motivation to work is different for people who come from Poland. There are not many possibilities to get money for university there. People who are coming over are from smaller towns, small villages. First of all they have this great motivation to get to the cities to study. But since their families are not able to help them, they have a great motivation to find something, anything, to pay for the university. It is hard work, but what are the options? Here people take out loans. Taking out a loan in Poland is . . . let's just say it's not easy. Everyone is worried where the money will come from.

So they come for the money, the experience, to improve their English. When you are picking fruit on the farms there are not always opportunities to speak English, but at some point you have to speak to the farmer. You can go into town, make contact with the language of this country, listen to the radio at night.

At night, most of us would sit around discussing things, drinking beer. Sometimes we would go with the farmer to the pub. We would make plans to go to London. During my second time here, when the soft fruit finished and before the apples started, we rented a car, four of us, and drove to

Snowdonia, to the Lake District, to Edinburgh. It was lovely, such lovely places. But this country, it's so expensive!

I remember first coming to England and being impressed by the solutions. Because even eight years after changing the system in Poland we did not have solutions like they did here. And everywhere – in the library, in the shop – people who were working in the service sector were nice. They were so open, they would speak with you. Our system: impossible. You have to ask so many times for someone to do the easiest thing, and they'll probably get upset first.

I was so impressed by the irrigation systems and all these fertilizers. Only the best farms had these systems in Poland. But the strawberries have a different taste – fresh and full of water. Polish strawberries weren't so big, they weren't so good-looking like the ones here, but in Poland the strawberries had more taste. Here, I was impressed at how fast they went from the field to the supermarket.

The work is difficult and the money is not so good. People here would rather get others to do the work. I think it is much more easy for a person in this country to find the work he wants to do. And the work they want to do is in an office or in a bank.

When Poland was communist, there were many people who wanted to come to this country and stay, just to get away from Poland. Now we come to this country, we get experience from the farms, we earn some money and we go back to Poland. Polish people want to apply what they've learned here to Poland.

*He's got a big smile and a large halo of curly hair. He's got a few tapes to listen to in the car as he moves about the country: some AC/DC, some Joe Strummer. His voice drawls.*

I'm from north of Christchurch, on the South Island of New Zealand, a little place called Waikuku. I'm a bricklayer by trade but I've been shearing sheep for four and a half years and I've been shearing alpacas for a good two years. Sheep are pig-ignorant. They just make your life hard. I know sheep are the lifeblood of my country, but give me alpacas any day.

I have a friend working with me. We've covered – no joke – about 5,000 miles on this trip. We'll do 250 miles in a day. Suffolk, Norfolk, Gloucestershire, Isle of Wight, Hampshire, Nottinghamshire . . . Yesterday we sheared fifty-six alpacas. The people all brought the animals to us. They put on a barbecue; we got to meet a few local characters, families, kids. If I have to shear more than twenty animals in a location I get paid per animal. Less than that and I get paid per job. One lady near Akenfield had seventeen alpacas she wanted sheared. People hear of us through word of mouth, really. We do a good job and that gets passed along. It's quite specialized work. In the UK you even have trouble finding local sheep shearers. A lot of the flocks aren't for wool production; they're for meat production. A lot of the time the fleece is just cut off and burnt. So you get New Zealanders and Aussies coming over to do the shearing. It's a hard job – in two months of shearing you do more work . . . well, more work than you might think it's worth.

My friend helps me get hold of them. Sheep you just do by yourself; with alpacas you tie them up, stretch them out. The fibre from their fleeces is much better quality than sheep. We go in with a rubber mat, restraining ropes, a pulling mechanism. Get the animal down, tie the front legs, stretch them out. Once their feet are bound, my friend holds the head and I get to work. You want to take the fleece from the saddle, from the neck, the places where the fibre is best. Fibres from all the other places can be used for felting. Then we go a bit further. We trim the toenails, trim the teeth. Give them a good personal-hygiene run-over. They deserve it! Some people who own alpacas are scared to get close to them. They'll call a vet in to sedate them before coming near. It's just all confidence. We can walk in and take care of them right away. I've got some good shears – an electric handpiece, a high make of brand. I can just plug them in and get to work. If you're sharp your days are easy.

Alpacas are becoming more popular because the fibre is second only to silk in quality. They've been breeding alpacas for fibre in South America for ages. They require less maintenance than sheep and, unlike sheep, they're quite intelligent. They can look after themselves and you're not out waiting for them to give birth on the coldest night of the year. Sheep give birth at the worst time. Alpacas wait for a lovely sunny afternoon. Sheep will just keel over and die for no reason. Alpacas – they're good. The males might spit at each other, and pregnant females might scream when you're shearing them, but they're fine. The females don't have a cycle, so you have to induce ovulation with them. You put a male in there with them to get them to start ovulating. Once pregnant they won't let a male get near. They'll spit in his face.

We see a lot of farms and from what I gather small-scale farming is not good. Sheep and cattle are so regulated – maybe that's why people are turning to alpacas. In New Zealand these strong niches are appearing – deer farms, ostrich farms. Anything's possible if you can get enough numbers. The problem for some is getting those numbers. Alpacas aren't cheap. We see people who have four – that's all they can afford. You won't see much change from 3,000 pounds for an animal that's near the bottom in terms of quality. And you might pay 80,000 pounds for a stud male. The top-price alpaca was selling for 550,000 US dollars on the world market.

As long as people have them in this country, I'll keep cutting. You're always a bit nervous with two sharp things cutting close to something worth so much. When you get a stud and you're floating around his back wheels with the shears out you want to really be careful. Don't want to lose its manhood. That's an investment lost. But you can't be too nervous.

Old-school farmers might look at alpacas and think it's piss in the wind. What would be the point? But the old way is not always the right way. Just because it's the way people have been doing it for 150 years in this area, doesn't mean it'll always be like that. The world progresses. Anything that can make life easier, more profitable, even if it's a strange animal like an alpaca . . . what could be wrong with that?

*Private Passions*

# DARREN CLARKE
## MAN WITH A METAL-DETECTOR, 39

*He stands in the middle of a wide, muddy field with his American-made metal-detector in his hand. It's an overcast day and he steps gingerly in his wellies over the humps of clingy soil. He has a determined look and he speaks quickly. He'd rather be listening for the high-pitched signals in his headphones. There is, he says, much more ground to cover today.*

A friend at work got me into metal-detecting. I've been doing it for ten years. I'm a train driver, see. I work for a freightliner that goes through Birmingham, Crewe, London, Felixstowe. This is just a hobby, just for the fresh air.

I get permission from the farmers and hope I might find a little something out there for them. I can come out into these fields any time of the year – September to April, really. My footprints are light; they don't disturb the land. The metal-detector is an American one, but it's a good one. I go fifty–fifty with the farmer. As long as you have a bit of respect for the crops and all that, the farmers are very good about it. Most of the landowners like me coming down here with my equipment. The rabbits probably do more damage than me. I wear wellies, so the worst that can happen is I stick to the land when it's wet. Besides, farmers are always looking for a way to make some money.

Normally I look for pottery shards. Up and down the field, up and down. There's a bit of Roman stuff in the area. But you don't get the pottery with the detector; you get the pottery by eyesight. I look for the pottery with my eyes, try to see where they were living. Hopefully they dropped something for us.

You have to put a lot of hours in. I might get the odd coin in the field up the road. I've got the headphones, so I'm constantly listening for a high-pitched noise. You can usually tell from the noise if it's good or bad. Iron is best, but you might find knives, thimbles, loads of bits of scrap lead, gun cartridge ends when they've been shooting. You put a lot of hours in and eventually you'll find something, but you'd be mistaken if you thought you could ever make a living from this.

Probably the best thing I've ever found is a bronze statue of a Roman dog, which is in Ipswich Museum. It got me 3,000 pounds. I found it on one of the fields, just up the road. I was chuffed. I was following a plane across the field – then I got the signal, took it up. It was probably six, seven inches down. It's bronze. Lovely. Second-century Roman. One of the men working on the farm saw me jumping up and down when I found it. The Ipswich Museum were interested in it and they would pay a good price for it, so me and the farmer decided to sell it to them. But I only found one metal dog in thirteen years. The Roman dogs don't turn up too often.

There's not really competition out here. Most of my farms are around Akenfield. When the soil turns over you never know what you'll find. Something will drop out. With a coin, you might not get to it until it's a few inches deep. One year it might be ten inches deep, next year the field will be turned and it'll be a few inches higher. A few inches higher the next year. It's history being churned up. Then one year it might come in range and I'll hear its signal. Who knows what's down there? You find Roman coins and some of them are worth nothing, they're so corroded. Even a silver Roman coin. You could buy one in the shop for about twenty pounds, a real top-quality one. We only split what's worth a bit of money.

I'll normally detect for about two hours, because after that your mind starts drifting and you can't keep concentrating. Two or three hours is plenty. A bit of fresh air, a bit of exercise. I've not been on all the fields around here but I feel fairly connected to the land. Eventually I'll get round to every field, hopefully. Thirteen years is a long time to be doing it. Some people give up after a year. You got to stick at it. I'll probably find something else this year. Whether it'll be worth any money or not, who knows? I'm guaranteed to find the odd coin or two, maybe a Roman brooch. They're normally broken. You pick one of those up and think, Couldn't those Romans have been a little more careful?

# TIM LODGE
## TURF SPECIALIST, 42

*He is thin, with a goatee and a deep Yorkshire accent. There is Yorkshire stone arranged around the pond in his garden. 'If I can't find Yorkshire in Suffolk,' he says, 'I'll bring Yorkshire to Suffolk. But I wrecked the suspension on my car getting the gritstone here.' Before growing interested in the natural world, he was passionate about the theatre. On our way to the pub, he quotes favourite lines from* Hamlet *while he drives the dark curves of the Suffolk roads. A tinge of performance enters into his voice as he delivers Polonius' advice: 'This above all: to thine own self be true.' At the pub his fiancée, Ursula, sits beside him, sipping white wine. She's bemused by all this passionate talk of turf. 'The stunning thing is that he gets phone calls from people crying to him, broken-hearted, like it's life or death,' she says. 'All they're talking about is their lawns. It's amazing. It's like someone died.'*

You have to be passionate about something. Back in 1986 or so, I'd got a degree in botany but I was passionate about theatre. I lived and breathed it. Turf wasn't anything on my horizon then. I was based up in the north of England, in Lancaster, and I needed a job. I was applying for theatre jobs and for botany jobs and I thought, Whichever one comes first I'll go down that road careerwise. My mum knew I was looking for a job around then, so she sent me a cutting out of the *Guardian* about this sports turf research institute. That's how it all started. Up to then I was like most people: I just didn't think about turf.

I did a research project on golf greens and then did a PhD with the University of Leeds on the structure of how golf greens work. When all the research work finished up, Suffolk Wildlife Trust offered me a job. Now I'm just about the only person in the country with a PhD in golf greens and fine turf. One other guy bodged together a thesis on soccer pitches – crap. A girl did a PhD on water diseases on turf – that was quite good. Mine was to do with irrigation: 'Irrigation and Fertilizing of Golf Greens in the UK'. When people decry the quality of further education, they always say, 'You can do a degree that is so crap it's called golf course management.' I always think, wait a minute . . . I did courses in life sciences, in geology, in surveying techniques. I use all of these things in the work I do now. It was really useful to me professionally. A few years ago, I read a book called *The Map That Changed the World*, about that bloke who made the map showing the geology of Britain, William Smith. He designed drainage systems, he was employed as a surveyor for the canal builders, and he made the map showing all the geology of Great Britain. You can see it at the Royal Geological Society at Piccadilly – it's ten feet high, five feet wide, shows all of Britain. It's just gorgeous, all perfectly clear. I relate to this guy. I was inspired by him!

Anyway, in golf course management you'd be learning how to deal with the bar staff. I'm dealing with turf. I cannot think of another crop that costs more money per square metre to maintain than a golf green. In some ways you're still farming the land. You're still growing a crop, taking care of it, you're just not into yield. The yield is the quality.

Golf internationally has got a bad press, and it's true that in the tropics it uses all the water and denudes the landscape and steals the village's water. But closer to home, at least the golf clubs maintain the bits that aren't played on. It does take maintaining, you see – maintaining the rough, chopping down trees, clearing scrubland. Between the fairways, the greens and the tees, you've got this heathland environment, which is so rare outside that and which the wildlife people are so fond of. The rabbits used to nibble the baby trees, so there would never be any trees. But when myxomatosis killed all the rabbits in the 1950s, it had a radical effect on the landscape of these places. They became overgrown. So the essential part of maintaining these heathland areas is to pull up all the trees. Gorse bushes, heather, that's OK. Dry grassland, that's super. But not trees.

If you were fortunate enough to have a patch of land over in east Suffolk on the sandy soil, then the procedures you'd have to do to get a really nice golf course wouldn't be that involved. The first thing you do is kill everything. Then you move it with bulldozers, move the soil around into the form you want it to be, then you re-establish what you're going to re-establish. The bulldozers and diggers destroy the existing vegetation, but if you know what you're doing you can recreate it. So it's not the end of the world.

If you look at the history of most golf courses in the UK, I would say that 60 per cent of them were established between 1890 and 1910. That's a lot of golf courses; there was a massive interest in golf then. There was a smaller burst in the 1920s, another burst in the 1970s, a small burst in the 1990s. Then it dried up. They just maxed out. Golf is primarily played by retired people and now there's more people retiring and people are living longer, so there may be a call for another expansion. But if you had land now, here, you'd be ill-advised to build a golf course with it.

I'm looking at polo as a business possibility. Polo is definitely on the rise. There's people who have got a lot of money and can afford the horses and the land, and therefore they want something to do with it. Polo fields – people want polo fields. To make a piece of ground fit, you're looking at getting it level, that's the most important thing. And polo fields are massive, at least 300 metres by 180 metres, because you've got to have space where you can run off the sides. The beginning of the polo season is roughly equivalent to the beginning of the cricket season, so it can be wet, almost unplayable. So you want your polo ground on somewhere better built or with nicer soil structure, so they can carry on playing right through from the start to the finish of the season. A lot of my work is involved with making sure these polo grounds are fit for play at the start of the season.

A farmer in Bury St Edmunds got in touch with me not so long ago to explore the possibility of turf production. That's very profitable, but you've got to have really nice soil for it. When I did my study for this chap I concluded it was going to be too much hard work for him, because the soil there is too heavy. You get a lot of coarser grasses coming in there. You can make turf for soccer pitches, say, but you wouldn't really want to use it. You want it ultra fine. The best kind of turf is the stuff that grows on sandy soil. One of the best turf farms is down the road from Akenfield. They've got these beautiful fields that look just like lawns. Fine grasses like festuca and agrostis, that's what you'll find in really top-quality lawns and bowling greens. They're very fine, so you get more shoots per square inch and that's what gives you the carpet-like surface. If you were fortunate enough to have a farm near there, on that sand, you could make turf that sells for two pounds a metre, or something like that. Two pounds a metre is a lot of money if you're thinking about the acreage. It's more than sugar beet or anything like that.

The growing amount of leisure time people have can only be good for me. The National Lottery has ploughed millions into sports fields and that's been good for people in my profession.

We build these sites, improve these places. I did a feasibility study in a village nearby. They were applying for a grant from the Football Foundation, which is part of the National Lottery that gives money to football, and they were talking 40–50,000 pounds for one football pitch. There's a lot of money floating around for this sort of thing. It's better than just leaving the land that used to be used for farming.

I do think the countryside is becoming prettier. The set-asides make a big difference. Biodiversity is the key word. You notice it around here: there are gaps between the crops and the side of the road and there's all this stuff growing there. Some see uselessness. But the mistake they always make is the idea you can just walk away from the land and it will turn into something beautiful. It doesn't work like that. All these beautiful sites were maintained in one way or another. Every bit of this country has had something done to it at some stage and it needs that ongoing process to maintain it. Like rabbits on heathland – if you don't want rabbits because they dig up your greens, you've got to do something else to maintain the heathland environment. Trees will grow if the rabbits aren't nibbling at them. First you get silver birch in, then you get the oak trees, and before you know it you've got forest.

## ALAN 'BUD' BUCKLES
### RAG RUG MAKER, 80

*He celebrated his eightieth birthday the week before the Harvest Supper. A few women from the village came to his council bungalow and made him tea. One gave him a bottle of whisky; another gave him a bottle of brandy. His voice is low and every word is delivered with equal weight. 'I was in the middle, one on each side. I thought to myself, I can't sit here for nothing, so I put my arm around one. Then I put my arm around the other one. I had two heads lying on my shoulder. I've done very well. I thought, This is the best birthday I've had since I was born.' Most Sundays he sits in the back pew of the Baptist chapel. The pews there surround the organist, who sits facing the elevated pulpit. Above the pulpit are the words* THE LAMB OF GOD TAKETH AWAY THE SIN OF THE WORLD *in bright red script. He gives me a slow thumbs-up when I see him there one Sunday.*

My nickname is Bud. I don't suppose there's half a dozen people what use that longer bit. Alan Hubert Buckles – that's a proper name. But Bud'll do me. I had it as a nickname practically ever since I been born. There was about nine of us and we all had nicknames. Hobs was one of my brothers, Sweat was another – he just died about two months ago. Once I went on a bus and someone said to me, 'Oh, you're going to see Harold?' I looked at him. 'Harold? Who do you mean?' He meant my brother. I don't believe all the while he was alive he didn't get called Harold a dozen times. I said, 'If you called him Sweat I'd know who you mean. But not Harold.' When you got a nickname, that stuck. If anyone was going to call you your proper name you wouldn't know which way to look. When they chuck me in the six-foot hole or the ten-foot hole, as the case may be, they'll use the long one. They don't want to use Bud. But when I'm down there they can please themselves with what they call me.

I had all my life in Akenfield. Only had about four little moves in the village since I was born till now. I used to go to Akenfield School, but I couldn't learn nothing so the old teacher pushed me out in the little old playground. It was about as big as this room. 'You go in the playground,' she said. 'You're no good in here.' And the next time she spoke, she said, 'The best thing you can do is go down to the shop and buy two pound of pig brains to make yours work.'

When I went to school I couldn't learn nothing. I couldn't learn to read and I couldn't learn how to write. But I made a rag rug. Easy. We would get a big bundle, pieces of wool and a bit of canvas. The wool always used to be all mixed up. Before you set to work and tried to do anything with it, you sorted it out. You made a nice little heap and you'd think to yourself, Right, I'll make a black top, more black down there, then you make yourself a rug. So you'd sort it all out and then you'd get a rug, put it on your lap, get a hooker and start making a rag rug. Every piece in that mat is tied.

If I wanted something else to do I'd find an old sack. I cut the sack open, made another rug with old coats and skirts. But I didn't want no jumpers! No, I wanted a stout skirt or something hard. A pair of trousers, a jacket. You can't do nothing with a jumper. But a good old black skirt or a grey skirt or a pretty frock or something like that is ample.

You have to find stout pieces. You've just got to have patience to do it. Patience and willpower. If you ain't got willpower you won't do nothing, will you? You can't just start the bloody thing and leave it alone. When I finish, if I got any little time left, I hunt round and find another sack. Cut the sack open and make another rug.

You were lucky to make a rug. Sometimes you had a hard job just to find the pieces to make it. You'd go get close to a woman and ask her if you could have her frock. She'd say, 'No, I still want it!' So that's it. You'd go to old jumble sales and buy an old frock for tenpence, a pretty frock, and they'd look at me and say, 'What you going to do?' Make a rug, I'd tell them. I'd sit down, you snip the whole lot and make a nice little rug.

A rag rug's a marvel. When I was a little one I couldn't find bloody much to do, so I found a pair of scissors and cut them. I was in a real mess when I finished but I done it. I done it and I cut it. And that's how I come to make my rugs so. But it's a long while ago I made my last rug.

I go to church, but not every Sunday. Sometimes I do if I get a bit bored of being here. Do I believe in God? Well, sometimes I do and sometimes I don't. If it weren't for God I wouldn't potter about like I'm doing today. I wouldn't know what to do. I can't write and I can't read. But I got a garden. I generally potter about in my garden.

One of my brothers is dead and another one is full of cancer. When they went to work they didn't know nothing about cancers and that sort of thing. As soon as they pack up work they were queer. They were queer and they kept going backwards and forwards to the hospital and that's it. They say smoking brings cancer but I don't know. I used to smoke a little. When the fags kept going up I said they're getting too dear for me. I packed up and I don't worry about it now. If you got cancer you got it. I went into the hospital for ten days. They didn't tell me what I got. They didn't tell me if I've got a cancer and I'm going to peg out in the next five or six months. I don't know. But they never told me – they kept X-raying me and one thing or another. I never heard how the X-rays got on. I don't want to. I done well, see. I don't worry what'll happen. It ain't no good worrying, because if you got it you got it and that's it. You've got to keep going. Get a spade, do a bit of digging. Take a big walking stick and walk out on the road somewhere.

There's a lot of people who said to me this year, 'Who dug your garden?'

I said, 'I did.'

They said, 'What made you dig it?'

I said, 'Look here, I dug it all myself because when I did it I didn't have to say thank you.'

When I finished it I didn't have to ask them how much did they want. But I ain't going to say I dug it all one day. I dug it for an hour. I'd go back. I'd sit down. I'd come out and give it another go. I've got some runner beans down there. I went down there on a Monday night with a pair of scissors, pulled them up, bunched all the rubbish up, put all my sticks in the drawer the same night. Pleased as punch to be outside doing a little. Fresh air.

This year I dug all my garden, pulled all my garden up. I got four rows of sweet williams. Beautiful flowers. There was two rows last year. This year I planted two more. I put my sweet peas in. I said to them, you've got two chances. Come back to me or go the other way. The sweet peas will come up. They'll come up.

## MAGGIE JENNINGS
### WALKER, 58

*She runs a bed and breakfast housed in a building once known as French's Folly, which has now been renamed French's Farm. There is a steep, twisting staircase at its centre and a lounge where the guests can sit by the fire and watch TV. Maggie has long hair, speckled with grey, and a tanned face and arms thanks to the walking tours. Outside the house is a collection of boisterous, mismatched chickens watched over by Brian, her partner. After the morning rush of breakfasts and teas for the guests, he claps his hands and leads them to their coop to be fed. She worked in radio for years and the BBC is on while she makes marmalade in the kitchen.*

At the BBC I was called a broadcast assistant, but I was actually producing the middle-of-the-day programme at local radio. Being in the provinces you got to do just about everything. Gradually the ethos changed. The managing editor was pushed out, the trailers were all zappy instead of being gentle rolling tunes. When they first went on air the tunes were taken from some of the old barge sea-shanties, played by the old barge skippers in Suffolk. I don't know how these things happen but they do. It's not just the BBC, it's everywhere. It's a young person's world, really.

I knew it was going to happen to me at some point, so one Easter when I was still working there I did a trial walking tour, a pilot one if you like, to see what the market was like. I advertised it and got thirty or forty phone calls – more than that, fifty or sixty – but I only took thirteen booked on the tour. I put up three in my house, three in my neighbour's house, several dotted around other bed and breakfasts. In those days I didn't read a map particularly well, so I did four walks and tried them each about four times before I took the customers. I did the tour and then went back to work. I did it just to see if there was a market. There definitely was. That's how I got into the walking business.

I just decided to go for it. I sold my car, added a couple of thousand and got a people carrier with the Tread Suffolk logo on it. Getting the footprint on the logo was the hardest thing. That's my logo: footprint on a map of Suffolk. I provide transport and I do full board in my house for up to six people. You never know who you've got coming. When I'm down, not feeling well or tired, it can be, 'Goodness, who have I got tonight? I hope they're nice.' There's always that slight worry. But we attract a certain type mainly by how we advertise. The majority come from word of mouth, our own website or the one bed and breakfasting book we're in. And you sort of read between the lines when you read my advert and it knocks out a lot of the sort of people I might not want here. We don't put televisions in the rooms. We don't put teas and coffees in the rooms. It's more a gentle come-into-our-home feel going on. If it was a boarding house I'd have to wear a hairnet and wrinkled stockings. It's our home, so we can't have people we're uncomfortable with.

In general, we get a staunch lot. They're well equipped, they're used to walking, so you don't have to question whether or not they've got a bottle of water or whether they've taken enough lunch to eat. There are couples and there are singles. I always tell everybody, do not come expecting to meet somebody – it's definitely not about that. Sometimes you get the person who thinks they can climb Everest, when in fact they couldn't walk four miles. Or you get people who don't wear the right kit: we've had somebody in miniskirt and sandals. Or you get people who wear reasonable stuff but it's not waterproof, or they have no hat for the wind. They think because it's Suffolk it's going to be a doddle. It's not, it's real walking. We've gone up to fourteen miles a day this year, and we're going to go up to seventeen next year.

It does make you look at the land differently. This sounds awful in my own county, but I quickly realized that if people are paying to come you can't just take them along the edge of a field. We have one or two really good walks right around here, but that's not quite good enough – they're around field edges. It has to be a knockout, it has to have the wow factor. It may be only three days, but it's their holiday and they have to go back thinking Suffolk is the most wonderful place and then come back again. I would think probably 50 per cent of them come back. Those who haven't been before don't realize it's as pretty. They think it's flat. I think they visualize Fenland, Cambridgeshire. One guy came from Lancashire – there's some lovely walking up there – and we took him to Ramsholt along the River Deben. The sun was out, and the river just glistens when the sun is out, it is just the most beautiful walk, absolutely breathtaking. He stopped and I thought there was a problem. He said he'd never seen anything as beautiful. He was quite choked! I found that a bit strange. It is beautiful, truly beautiful, but what he's used to is so much larger. His words to us were, 'You don't get this where I'm from.' The thing is, it takes you by surprise. When you take the car journey to where I'm taking them it's not wondrous. You're not passing superb lakes, glistening mountains, lovely valleys, you're just driving along roads with houses and trees and fields. The landscape subtly changes. But then I park, and they find we're full of beautiful rivers, creeks and estuaries.

We are in a big walking culture now. There are hundreds of walking companies out there and it is a little bit culty, if you like. It's a bit fashionable to wear the right gear. It has lost its image of 'the rambler' always in red socks, red pom-pom hat, seventy-plus and with a rucksack. The ramblers do a terrific amount of good work, but that was the image. You still do get a few farmers who don't keep their paths open. But the more you walk, the more countryside is kept open. You walk past people's gardens, sometimes through people's gardens. Those are people, at least I've found, that enjoy the walkers going alongside or through it. They keep their fences low so you can see and enjoy what they've planted. And they plant the most enjoyable gardens.

I met my Brian on one of these walks. I know, I know, having said you never meet anyone . . . But I met him there one year. Later he started emailing me these great long letters. I kept it going and a few months later we met up. He's very different from me. I'm a get-up-and-doer and he's a thinker. He's thinking deeply all the time. I'm thinking of five things and doing them at the same time. He's very much my foil. I get very tired in the evenings; he paces himself much more. And we both share a love of a good pint! I do like my beer. I used to make it at home at one point, when I had an old Belling cooker when the children were young. I used to get the barley, soak it and put it out in the sun, roasted it to turn it into malt in the oven, ground it all up – goodness knows how I did all of this – mashed it. I've forgotten all the expressions, but I put it in this jam kettle thing with the hops and made something as nigh on as a pint of Adnams.

We've got a lovely vicar at the church. I know her well, and I go to the odd sort of thing there. I've made dozens and dozens and dozens of scones for them. But going to church is something I got out of the habit of doing a long, long time ago and I haven't got back into it. The services are at ten o'clock and I'm usually still serving breakfast . . . That's a lame excuse, because if I really wanted to go I suppose I would just leave Brian doing breakfast. I suppose it's just very hard for me to go to the church, because my son Andrew is buried in the graveyard. His service was held in the church. It was the most beautiful funeral. We had some very strong singers, and all my friends and people who had supported me throughout my life came. I'd had a very hard time with Andrew, he was ill from about ten. That was when things began to show. At that age, though, you put it down to being just adolescence creeping on. It was silly things, like he'd leave a whole week's worth of packed lunches in the bottom of the bag to go mouldy. He would not eat anything. It was prattish behaviour and I just wanted to shake him and belt him. I thought, For goodness' sake, get a grip. What are you eating? It never occurred to me there was a deeper problem. Eventually we learned that it was paranoid schizophrenia he was beginning to grow into.

He was twenty-five when he died and he was ten when he began. It came creeping up with this dreadful behaviour. He got older. He was getting a job, going and living in a flat and then falling down and really falling through the bottom. By then he was nineteen, twenty. By then he was a very strange young man. Although I was his mother and loved him to bits, I had little to do with him; he was an adult and he was living this strange undercover life I knew nothing about. There was an episode where he got into trouble with the police and at that point he was diagnosed. After that it was easier to be more supportive because I knew there was something desperately wrong. The next four years he lived in a home and towards the end he used to phone me and say, 'You know, this won't go on for ever. I can't live like this. I've got to do something about it.' I used to cry, try not to but cry, and try to talk him through it. A year before his death he was still at the stage that whatever I said to him he'd grasp on to, and I remember on one occasion saying, 'You can't drive because your tablets are not stable enough but you could get yourself a bicycle and you could read up on cycling and perhaps go for cycle rides and not see anybody.' I told him that because his paranoia was so bad.

He had a wonderful few months planning this bicycle trip. He bought the tent, the maps. He comes over and sees Brian and says, 'This is what I'm going to do. How do I get there?' Thetford Forest is where he wants to go. But once he'd done all that he couldn't put it into action because the paranoia was so bad. That's how the brain works. All the neurons are missing. So we had all these dreadful phone calls where he used to say, 'I'm going to have to do something about it, Mum.' And that was very, very hard, terribly hard.

On the last night we were full with bed-and-breakfast guests. He turned up very, very late. I was in my pyjamas, sleeping in the annexe. The house was full of guests but I caught him as I was coming out of the annexe because I heard the car pull in. I wondered what on earth it was. He was driving and I was worried he wasn't sober, but he was. He'd been drinking a lot of coffee and he was just shaky. He took our hose. He made up this cock-and-bull story about how he'd hit something with his car and needed it. Of course, it was an excuse, an excuse to take my hosepipe. I thought he'd killed somebody, knocked somebody down. I was frantically trying to find out, to keep him here while Brian popped out to the car to see if there was blood or anything like that.

It might sound very strange to come and take a hose at eleven o'clock at night but for a paranoid schizophrenic it's not so strange. He used to turn up at two in the morning and do funny things. Or he'd phone me in the middle of the night and be on the phone for three hours. So it wasn't so odd. He put the hose in the car and before he left he kind of groaned, sort of went *ohh* and hugged me. He said to Brian, 'Take care of my mum.' And then he left. That's when we realized it wasn't anything to do with damage on the car or cleaning the car. We tore off after him. Of course I had my pyjamas on. We lost a minute or two. It's not real, is it? It's not real at all, you keep thinking. I can remember faffing about and trying to put my jeans on over my pyjamas and I'd put on so much blooming weight I couldn't put them on. We tore off and followed the route all the way back to his house, but we couldn't find him. In fact he was just down the lane.

I didn't sleep. I kind of knew. On the other hand, he might have thought he was going to do it and then he might not have done it. He was very, very sick. So anything could have happened. He could have bungled it. In the morning I was walking the dog over there because we had got six guests in. I heard Brian open this window and there was a blooming great black crow in this room. So I just thought, Andrew's dead. It seemed to me a clear sign. The police arrived and said they'd found him.

At the time I didn't want a soul to know. I had been here only a couple of years. I didn't know so many people. The phone calls and letters I got were from friends elsewhere. I used to drive miles out of my way so I wouldn't go past where it had happened. Because it was a suicide, local people didn't gossip – or if they did, it was neighbourly and close; I was left well alone. And I was happy to have a woman dealing with it. I had met Betty before, at the village hall when I was catering a funeral, and she was particularly supportive.

It sounds really hard. I don't mean it to, but if I could have had my healthy son I would never have wanted it to happen. But he was so desperately ill. His head was so mixed up that it was best he went. Bless his heart, he took it into his own hands and did it and saved us all the heartache. I don't know how much people know about paranoid schizophrenia – people with this illness can function, but they're very frustrated people, both in mind and in body. And you do hear of these dreadful things where they go out and do dreadful things. And they could kill or rape. I'm not saying Andrew could do anything like that. You just don't know. You don't know what might or could have happened in the future. He spared his whole family that. I have my tears when I tell the story but we're very grateful to him for doing that. Very brave.

He's buried in the Akenfield churchyard. Andrew has good neighbours. On the anniversary of his death, we went and poured a pint of beer on his grave. And we had one ourselves.

*The Churchyard*

## PEGGY COLE
### PILLAR OF THE VILLAGE, 70

*Her mother, she says, was 'hard working and quite a big woman, like I am today'. She has written books about Suffolk sayings and forgotten words which are sold above the bread at the local garage. She had a starring role in Peter Hall's 1974 film version of* Akenfield *and has travelled the world making after-dinner speeches about the book and movie. Her garden, with its thirty-five varieties of vegetables, was open to the public for years. She has two sons in the police force and even now they ask why she is always travelling back to Akenfield to attend Harvest Suppers and other events. They warn her against getting involved in all that work again – committees and fund-raisings. When she put her house up for sale, one shed was full of eighty gallons of homemade wine. The deep freeze was packed with preserves. 'We advertised a garage sale when I left,' she says. 'A lot of people who came weren't worried so much with what was in the garage as what we had put in the skip: old pieces of tools, old pictures, flowerpots.' After selling up she moved to a nearby town. Even her car resisted leaving Akenfield. After driving past the last farm in the village the fan belt snapped.*

My father worked on the land. He was a horseman and an agricultural worker. My mother worked as a servant at the old psychiatric hospital at Melton. She was a maid. We lived in what was called a tied cottage, a cottage what go with the farm. If the farmer don't like you or you have a row, you'll have to get out. Sometimes the wife would work for the mistress of the farm and if they fell out, again, you'd have to go. The boss would say, 'My wife has had a row with your wife and they don't agree and you'll have to get out and I want you out within a fortnight.' If you hadn't got another job you had the bailiffs come and put your furniture out by the side of the road. That was in the early 1930s, when it was very bad.

My father had Parkinson's disease and after a while he started shaking a lot. But they didn't understand what he'd got and the farmer told him, 'You're getting too slow, Fred. I think you'd better go.' My father was very upset. He come home and told my mother. There was four of us then. My mother saw another job in the paper near Cambridgeshire, which was a heck of a way to us. We thought we were going to the end of the world – it's only about fifty miles away. We went on this other farm and my father was still not getting any better and that went on for another year. They had a cow who produced milk for the farmhouse. I used to go milk it in the mornings before I went to school and when I come home, because my father had lost his grip and he didn't want the farmer to know.

One day the farmer come round and caught me milking it. He said to my father, 'What's the meaning of this? What's the kid doing milking the cow?'

He said, 'I'm sorry, I can't grip.'

'Right,' the farmer said, 'you get out then. You're no good to me.'

So, my mother and father looked in the papers again and he saw a listing at the farm at Akenfield, where he first worked when he came out of the army. They were advertising for a farm worker. Mother wrote to them and said he wasn't very well but he could still do a decent day's work and they'd got a cottage and would they consider having him back? They said yes, they would. We were back there.

I was about eight or nine then. I used to go help on this farm on weekends, collecting eggs and doing odd jobs. One day I went with my father. He was on a bicycle and he lost his balance and went into the ditch. He just couldn't get up. So the farmer said, 'If that's how you are you're no good to me. You must get out.' So three times they had to get out of cottages. You had to pack up all your belongings in a horse lorry. Everything, your bed, your linen, your settee and chairs, everything you'd got in the house – you had to pack it up in boxes the best you could. Even if you'd got a shed outside you had to take that down with your garden tools in and pack that all in. And it all went into one of those big cattle lorries. They couldn't afford a proper furniture lorry.

Mother said, 'Well, we're in a mess now. We'll never be able to get into another farm cottage.' She said she was going to see the minister at Akenfield because he was on the council and they were building the council houses along the street. This Pastor Baker, he was a dear old boy, and we got the last council house in Akenfield. That was in 1948. It was lovely. There was three bedrooms and electricity and a bathroom and a flush toilet. We'd never had that anywhere else. It was always a bucket-and-chuck-it toilet. So that was my father and mother's lives.

When I left school at fourteen, in 1949, I got a job in the shop and I was quite chuffed. I used to go round the village with a tray bike, taking groceries around. There weren't a lot of entertainment. The church, you see, is where we used to meet. We'd have lantern shows with a big sheet up in the church. It was mostly about Jesus in his country and the other lands, Egypt, things like that. That was all to do with a bit of religion. For us that was something to look at.

There was so much fruit-picking work in Akenfield back

then on the land. We used to go start fruit picking the goose-berry season in June, right through to November. The women could go and earn. When I first started, my children had got bigger and went to the junior school. I went to work on the farm in the house. There was a lady nearby in Letheringham and she wanted somebody in the house, so I went to work for her, two or three years. Well, then they had pigs. They started up a pig company that supplied pigs every month, so they asked me if I would go work outside with these little pigs. You had to cut the teeth out and look after them. Then I got so I was castrating these pigs and I worked there I suppose eight or nine years, then I got a bit fed up. I thought, Why should I keep doing this? I saw the job adver-tising at St Audrey's – carers, nurses – so I went there, and that's where I finished.

Before I went to the pig farm I used to pick. I'd go with Mrs Frost, Peggy Buckles, Bud's sister, Clare Harris, Mrs Branton, Mrs Osbourne. We met in the mornings, called at the shop, got anything we wanted to take up to drink. Sometimes the chil-dren would come up in the evenings in the summertime, so we might have called in the shop and got them some crisps so we had them ready up in the fields for when the children got there. And we'd just talk about what's happening in the village: who'd gone off with somebody or who'd died. Or how do you cook your pie – what pastry do you use, we'll have to try that. When jam season come along, oh, I did my jam last night, it wouldn't set. Somebody would say, 'You put too much water in, you should try it this way.' That was quite a good conversation on the country life. We never discussed much about the news. We never heard much about the news then. This would be early 1960s.

Televisions were just then coming into the village. Mr Weston was the first farmer to have one, then Mr Kitson. My brother, Ronnie, worked on the farm up near where I lived then. One weekend he said to me, 'I'm going to do a surprise for Dad – I'm going to get him a television.'

I said, 'Ronnie, you'll never be able to afford that.'

He said, 'I've been saving up.'

Back then you had to ask the council if you could put an aerial on the roof, so he went to the council, and they came out and looked. My father said to my brother when he come home, 'There's been a bloke outside looking round the house this morning, don't know what he's on.'

'You don't have to worry about him,' Ronnie said.

The next Saturday he had this television come. I think Ronnie paid about sixty pound, and the rest he paid off eventually. Oh, my father was absolutely thrilled. He loved horse racing, and anything to do with sport. I can see his face now – it was wonderful.

People thought, Oh, they're a poor family but they've got television. They soon heard how Ronnie had put his money down and paid for it. In the next month or so you suddenly saw the television aerials going up.

We didn't know much about the world. The big event in the village was the church fête, which was always in June, St Peter's Day. I used to run that for years. Then the Baptist chapel had their anniversary, always the first Sunday in July. Everybody had new clothes and hats for the chapel. There would be talk in the fields – have you been to the shop? Have you got your new hat or dress? Sometimes we'd go on the bus on Saturdays to Ipswich to find some new clothes and the women would work hard all year to have their children dressed up just smart for that.

We'd talk to each other about pregnancies, but not sex. If any girl got into trouble, there'd be a bit of gossip. One or two were known for their gossip. One woman, she had a nickname: the News of the World, we called her. We shall hear what happened overnight!

The older women would talk to the younger women. They

used to say to the ones who were getting married, 'You wait, you'll have a lot to sort out. You'll only have so much money to spend. You'll have to have your tin with so much put away,' and try and tell them all that and lead them on a good way of life. It was a place where that kind of information could be passed. You don't learn about some things in the village. In the fields you could learn.

When I had my first miscarriage I didn't know what was happening to me. I had an awful pain. We kept two pigs at the bottom of the garden in a pen. One day one of them got out and I was going down the garden path and this pig come up the path and I tried to shoo it back. It hit me right in the stomach and threw me over. I never thought no more of it. I got back up, but that night, you see, I had awful pain.

I said to my husband, 'I've had ice cream and that's upset me.'

Then I started to get so much pain, so he said, 'I think you'd better go to bed.'

When I got to bed I noticed I was bleeding quite badly. I said, 'I think you'd better go get Mother and ring up the doctor.'

He went down and got my mother and she cycled up with the neighbour and the doctor came. I never saw her but I was nearly six months and that was a little girl they told me. They put her in a little box and I had to go away to hospital. So that was quite a bit to talk about, you know, in the fields. They all used to listen to me.

Whether that was the pig done it, I don't know. I always remember that the women were kind and sorry to hear. I'd got the pram and everything, you see. I said to them, 'Whatever you do when you're having a baby, don't get the pram before.' I told them this out in the fields. We used to talk about things like that.

There was an old lady who I picked fruit with, older than the others, whose job was to help lay out the dead. One day out in the fields she said, 'Peggy, I'm getting old. Will you come help me with the next person to die?'

'Well', I said, 'all right, if you think I could help you.' Good God, I thought, I hope you don't have anybody yet.

I think within a month somebody did die, and she said, 'Will you come?' It was getting to be quite a lot for her. You had to wash them and turn them over, you know. She said, 'This is what I do. And when anything happens to me you'll have to do this, you know.'

It was a man. The first time I had ever seen a dead man.

She said, 'Now, the first thing is we've got to wash him. All over.' And I felt a bit embarrassed for the poor old man. She said, 'We must block up all the holes.' So I turn him up, you see, and plugged all the holes. Oh, I thought, this is a funny business. 'It's because they might leak,' she said, 'so you got to do that.'

Then we had to wash and tie the feet up. She had bandages in her little box. We put the hands across the chest, you know. She used to put pennies on the eyes, but very often they were closed. Little plugs went up the nose. Ears and all, I did. Sometimes we'd put the false teeth in if they were there. If not, we didn't. And then put a clean shirt on them, and that was all and that was ready then for the undertaker, for him to come do it.

This all took place in the old man's house, in his bedroom. Right where he died. If he died at home you just went into the bedroom and done it. The people who were there would get you water and bring you the things. I had a little bag. I kept everything in there that I wanted: talcum powder, bandages, scissors. Mostly people died in their own houses. We used to put a piece of rubber sheeting quickly under the bed in case there was an accident, you know, before we started that was. Nowadays they just come and take them away and do them at a funeral parlour.

I don't know why I was chosen. I got on well with this woman who used to do it. I remember my husband's father was very ill and he died. I was there when she come and she said, 'Peggy, would you give me a hand with this?'

And I said, 'Yes, all right, I'll help you.'

When she told me I will be the one to help her in the future I didn't have much choice! I thought, Somebody's got to do it. Who else is going to do it?

You realize that a lot of them are out of their misery. They're at peace. There was a look on a lot of those faces. You do see that when people change. I knew them all. I thought, Poor old boy, poor old lady. There was one lady who I knew who lived with her daughter, and she died in the chair the night before. Just like I am here. The daughter put an eiderdown and a blanket over her and left her and she rang me the next morning.

She said, 'Peggy, Mother's died. Can you come and do for her?'

I said, 'I'll be up in about twenty minutes.'

When I got up there, the daughter said, 'She's in the chair under the eiderdown.'

I said, 'Didn't you put her on the bed?'

She said, 'No, should I have done?'

Of course, because she'd set; the rigor mortis had set in. I thought, My God, what am I going to do? So the daughter got all the water for me to wash her with and then she went out of the room. I thought, My godfathers. I had to pull her out of the chair and tip her on to the bed. Of course she was still stiff, sitting in the chair. Dear old girl, I thought; well, I couldn't help it – I had to pull her legs out, pull her arms. Crack, crack. Oh dear, I'd never had that experience before! I hope I never have to do anything like that again. I managed to get her straight, though her knees were still a bit up.

The daughter asked, 'Did you have a job?'

I said, 'Yes, I believe I did. A pity you never put her on the bed.'

I daren't tell her what I'd done – I thought that would upset her. I rung the undertaker and told him what had happened.

'My God,' he said, 'you should have hit her with a hammer.'

I couldn't have done that. But that was the only one I had to do like that. After a while new rules came out, and undertakers came and took them away, so I didn't have to do that no more. I suppose I done about twenty in the village.

My husband died very sudden. I found him in bed. I don't know what there is but as soon as I woke up that morning there is a horrible silence everywhere. You know, you can feel it, there is a sense. I knew there was something wrong and I looked at him and I could see he had died. The undertakers took him right away. I didn't do nothing. But there is a sense when you go into a room where anybody's dead. There's that quietness.

And the dead look so peaceful, so often. People go back to the chapel of rest after a couple of days. The bodies have had time and they do look very peaceful. I suppose it's more heart-breaking if you've got to see somebody, like one of your children, or a teenager or something. That is a bit heart-rending. But an older person, you think they've had their time and that's that.

For me it's now less of a mystery. I often think – I'm seventy – I often think, Cor, I better wash up before I go to bed in case anything happen to me tonight. I must tidy up a bit. I'd hate to leave a mess. Oh, you dizzy fool, I think, you won't have to worry anything about it.

I used to help my husband Ernie to dig the graves. Or I should say I used to help fill them in. I didn't do the digging out. I used to help him shovel the soil back in. While we were filling the graves in, Ernie would always say to me, 'Oh, I don't want to lie here in the cold.' He said, 'I'd rather be burnt up.'

I said, 'Yes, I would too.'

I think a time will come where there won't be room to bury

people. They're now burying in Akenfield on top of people who have been buried there 100 years. I don't like that thought somehow. If you're burnt up, that's it. Very often you'd have to do a double grave and you'd come on to the other coffin, you see. Ronnie used to help him sometimes and if Ronnie got on to that other coffin he was out of that grave like a shot. In case that fell in, you know, or it had rotted or something. I wouldn't ever get in. I would go after the funeral and I'd sometimes help him push dirt into the hole. Very often I done that, but I didn't ever get down in the hole and dig them out. They had to be a certain level and shape. Nowadays it's machines that do it. There aren't many people who could dig a grave.

I do believe there's an afterlife. If you didn't believe, then life isn't worth living, really. You've got to think you're going to a better place. You meet your loved ones in the end. I shall be cremated and my ashes will go with my husband. His ashes are up there in the churchyard, not far from my mum and dad.

## CHARLES LEVERETT, OBE
### WIDOWER, 97

*He is walking me through his house. 'There is nothing else to see in this room,' he says after showing off a camphor trunk carved by Indian craftsmen in the dining room. It's what kept his clothes safe from the red ants of Dar es Salaam and the moths of Kenya as he travelled in the colonial service. In the same room there is a set of delicate herons carved from the tusks of rhinos, and photos of water buffaloes staring sullenly at the cameraman. On his way to the kitchen he picks up a hand-carved mallet and beats it against a drum. 'Now this here,' he says above the pounding, 'this is what we used to do in Goa.' In the cold front room there is a piano, a landscape of the River Deben near Woodbridge, and a grandfather clock he bought from the neighbours for two pounds. Between two more tusks of rhinoceros ivory there is a small gong, which he strikes with the mallet. 'That's how you would call someone to a meal,' he says. 'But we didn't use it often. You knew when you were hungry out in the colonies.' He walks up the stairs to his bedroom with its two single beds, one smoothed and untouched and the other only slightly rumpled. A woman's hand mirror is on the bedside table, beside it a brush with a lone fingerprint in the dust on the handle. 'I still sleep here. I haven't changed anything.'*

A lot of people express surprise that I am this old. Sometimes I'm just as surprised. But there we are. I was born in a small village in Norfolk called Alby. I started working on what was then the Midlands and Great Northern Railway. After about seven years I decided to enlarge my horizons a bit and I joined the Colonial Service, which ran railways in all the colonies – such as they were.

We haven't got any colonies left now. It's disappointing in a way, because so many of us spent our lives in the various colonies teaching them to run the railways, run all the services one would expect. Now we've left a few semi-educated ones in most colonies who have got political control, and what a mess they're making of it. They're all in debt, and law and order, I think, is not anything like it was when we were there.

In 1931 I was posted to what was then Tanganyika, on the east coast of Africa just south of Kenya, right on the Equator. In those days there was no aircraft. You had to go by sea and that took thirty or so days. Tanganyika had been German East Africa before the First World War, and it was never an actual colony as such. It was a mandated territory. Those countries belonged to or were ruled by countries who were our enemies during the war, so of course we just took over. I joined the army in the Second World War and served in the desert in the Middle East and in the Madagascar Landing. Madagascar, that great island in the Indian Ocean, was French – that's why we had to take it, you see, because the Vichy French were, as far as we knew, allowing the Jap subs to refuel, and they were sinking our ships in the Mozambique Channel. So we had to take it. It wasn't difficult. Then, of course, we had to deal with the Italians, who then ran Abyssinia. They started invading Kenya from the north. I was King's African Rifles, and we had to stop them. But that was not difficult, because the Italians didn't really want to fight. Their heart wasn't in it. After that we went up to the desert, against Rommel, which was a different kettle of fish.

When the war ended I accepted a transfer, a promotion, to Palestine, which was a mandate we looked after. I was running a railway that came down and connected to Egyptian railways. I spent two years in Palestine, mainly in Haifa and Jerusalem, but up to Lebanon to the north too. Then I came back to East Anglia.

I remember the day I met my wife, Marjorie. I had been on British Railways. When I was offered the post in the colonial service I went to the local manager, who kindly relieved me of all duties. Naturally when I came home on my first leave I went to the headquarters in Lynn to thank this man for taking over for me and tell him how I was getting on. Among the two or three girls in the headquarters was Marjorie, whom I hadn't met before, though I knew her father because he was also railways. It went on from there. I was almost due to sail again so we decided it would be better not to rush into things and then regret it. We'll see if it lasts two and a half years, which was my next tour. And it did. We existed on letters and air-mail cards and things like that.

In these letters I wrote to her, I would tell her about the animals of Africa. It's difficult to write to somebody about somewhere they've never been. In those days there were always little animal incidents. I used to shoot for the pot. Buck and dik-dik and small animals. Dik-dik is a little deer. I never shot a big animal, though I've seen plenty of them. She could tell me local Norfolk news. It worked all right. After two and a half years we were still practically strangers so we had to start again, you see, before we were married.

We married and she went back with me to Africa, and then to Palestine, until the terrorism got so bad we had to evacuate all the women and children. We were parted for some long time. She came back home to her people and lived in Lynn. So the first ten years of our married life was spoilt with war. My wife was in the services as well, she was a field auxiliary nurse, but she didn't nurse much in the last war. She did mostly secretarial work. She was secretary to a general in Africa. As we were well established in Nairobi, it didn't really matter where I was posted to. She was stable and had a house in Nairobi. I was involved with railways all the time. I was first commissioned into the First Battalion King's African Rifles, which was an infantry battalion. But when it was known that I'd been all my life involved with railways I was pulled out and posted to Royal Engineers, to work on railways the army had taken over.

For most of our time in Palestine we lived on the slopes of Mount Carmel in Haifa, overlooking the Mediterranean. The only bad thing was the terrorism. You just didn't take chances. Some of my colleagues were shot. The railways were one of the best targets, one of the easiest for terrorism, so it was nothing unusual to have a train blow up. They used to manufacture a little bomb to put under the track in the dark, which blew a hole in the track. That was about all that was needed to derail a train. Why there was so much trouble while we were there was it had been Palestine, part of Arabia, if you like, until Hitler started kicking out his Jews, who regarded Palestine as their natural home. They all wanted to come to Palestine. Every old Greek shipowner rigged up any old ship he could find and filled them up at Marseilles and sent them to mainly Haifa. I was involved in trying to find somewhere to put them. There were thousands. Fortunately the British army was then leaving Palestine, because trouble died down so we were able to put them in old army camps. They were mostly women and old men, because Hitler had killed a lot of the young men. I've been involved in history a little bit, haven't I?

I served out my time there in 1948. I was offered Sierra Leone on the west coast of Africa, which I didn't fancy much. I had never been to the west coast, but I didn't think it was as nice as the east coast. Soon I was transferred to Kenya, which was just what the doctor ordered, because I had been in Tanganyika, which was adjacent. I spoke Swahili. They all spoke the same language, that bloc of Africa, and I worked out the rest of my time there. Latterly we used to fly. That was easy. In the older days, when you went by sea, you doddled around on old coal-burning ships and called at ports you probably wouldn't nowadays. It made life interesting.

Kenya was a very nice place to live, especially in Nairobi. Sunday afternoons our entertainment was getting the car and driving out to the plains to see the lions and elephants all in their natural state, and provided you didn't disturb them and left them alone, then they left you alone. I met an elephant in the road. We looked at each other and he went his way, I went mine. Just like that. My wife entered into it all. The things you really had to be careful with were malaria and dysentery and what we called black water, which is when you had malaria so badly your kidneys broke down and bled. It wasn't very common. Don't forget I'm talking about forty years ago. You looked after yourself; you had to. Otherwise, you could easily get ill and invalided out.

I finally decided to come back to England because of retirement age, which in the colonies was lower. You didn't stay much after sixty, except if you wanted to you could retire there. We came home from Africa in 1961 by taking a round-the-world trip. Instead of coming our normal way up the Red Sea, Suez Canal and so on, we went due east through Panama. We went right round the world by sea, which you can't really do now because there aren't any ships. Easy enough to do it by air. We saw how the rest of the world lives. Our final trip home took us to the Far East, Madagascar, Australia, New Zealand, Panama . . . We were at sea for about two months.

We tried to find a place in Norfolk, because all my relatives are still there. Suffolk was the next best thing. When I bought this place the school next door had been the village hall, which nobody took any notice of. I bought it too. It cost me quite a bit, but I sort of renovated it. Eventually I sold it. It's been a private house for many years. The big house next door on the other side was the rectory and the village was much the same as it is now, except this area here was the rector's meadow, where he kept his ponies and things.

When we moved back here, we had a ceremonial burning of our letters. We had a bonfire down there in the garden. We had both kept all our letters over this two and a half years. It was just Marjorie and I there. We had no children. So there is no evidence of all the words we wrote each other. Even now I don't regret burning her letters, though they might have been pleasant to read. It was a ceremonial burning. I probably saved the stamps, which had come from different countries. I think we just sort of looked at it and let it burn out.

I took an interest in the weather. This East Anglian weather is a great hobby. I've got close to it. Whether it's fine or cloudy or frosty or rainy, I measure the rainfall. I used to send my rainfall readings to the *East Anglian*, but three or four years ago they said they didn't want it any more, so I just stopped. But I still do it for myself. I even measured this morning. We had an inch of rain yesterday in twenty-four hours up to this morning. Having lived in different climates you become quite involved with weather.

I only am engaged with my own couple of acres here. I fenced off a cage to keep the rabbits off and used to grow vegetables, but since my wife died I'm afraid I've let it go quite a bit. I have a chappie who cuts my grass, otherwise the weeds and things are getting me down. I find I go out with good intentions. The spirit is willing but the flesh is weak. I'm afraid I don't do much. I used to keep all this immaculate. The place is big enough that it just doesn't matter, really. If you leave a thing long enough it will die off.

I never thought I would grow old in a small English village.

I've just been philosophical about things. You can't do anything about them so you might as well accept them. Certain things like whether you accept a transfer to serve in different places. If it was a promotion, you took it.

In this village there is an opportunity to go your own way and do what you like without anyone interfering or showing any interest. The soil is good, a bit heavy. I sit here at night with about half a dozen rabbits outside. I haven't got a gun these days; I don't shoot. They can come and eat my grass as much as they'd like. In fact, I've let the beds go quite a bit because I just can't cope. I'm getting too old. I don't attend church. My people were Wesleyans and so we always attended services as boys but I haven't . . . If the church ever wanted anything and I could do it, I did it. I kept on the right side of my conscience.

Marjorie died eight years ago. I'm still looking after myself, teaching myself to cook. Everything is as it was. I'd never done any cooking. I'd hardly made a cup of tea, but when you're faced with it and have got to do it yourself, then you must get on with it. I suppose there's a certain legacy from many years ago when we young men went to Africa and had to look after ourselves. A certain amount of that is left in me.

It's no fun being a bachelor at my age. You are, I suppose, growing outside society. It's not necessarily lonely. One or two people up the road entertain me a bit. Although I can't entertain in the house, I take them up to the pub sometimes. The people who live in the schoolhouse, I'm told, keep an eye on my curtains or my lights at night to see how I am. I would do the same for them. I don't want to get too much in anybody's pocket. I'm too old to be invited into anybody else's. But I've lots of memories and thoughts.

My wife was cremated at Ipswich and her ashes are in what they call the Spring Garden there. I'm not over-sentimental about things, because when you go around the world for some years you sort of regard everything as inevitable and you accept it. It's no good making myself unhappy just because I'm alone. I shall be cremated as well. That's in my will. And my ashes will be put anywhere they like. I shan't know. I might be scattered near the rabbits in the garden. That's a thought. Most of the trees near the garden are big willows we planted. Even those poplars my wife and I planted. In fact, I'm amazed at how big things can get. I'm quite close to nature, as it were. It gives me a certain interest to see what does what and how. Birds and animal behaviour. Pheasants will come to the back door. Rabbits. Hares, no. But squirrels. I've got a squirrel who comes quite close. Fish in the pond. We get heron in. That is the sort of thing that strikes you – nature continues.

## RONNIE BALLS
### CHURCHYARD CARETAKER, 67

*He sits in his front room, surrounded by paintings and photos of his favourite type of horse, the Suffolk punch. His collection has grown over the years from birthdays and Christmas gifts. He is one of the few bachelors in the town and still lives alone. 'I never went courting much,' he says. 'I used to love doing my job so I never worried about that. I would begrudge the time if I had to go out with anybody. I used to love doing grass cutting, I used to love being on my mower. They always tell me when you get married you're trapped.'*

I started working when I left school at fifteen. I would lead horses, muck pigs out, drive tractors, anything like that. We all mucked in with the men. We all done things like topping the sugar beet. There was hedge cutting and grass cutting, because there weren't the clippers like there is now. They used to do it all by hand. We'd be topping the beet one day and if you cut your finger you wouldn't know how you done it. The beet had ice all over it that froze your hand and if you cut your finger you wouldn't know until you stopped for food and seen your finger all blood.

When we first went on the farm we had very bad winters. We don't get the severe winters now like we used to do. Sugar beet season is September to November and even towards Christmas and a lot of people now want to get them out before the bad weather comes, the snow and ice. They use the machines. That's all modernized. There's one skilled man on a farm doing everything now, ploughing and combining with a tractor.

When I first went on there, there used to be about nine to ten men. We'd all sit together when we ate. Sometimes we'd come home if we lived near, but sometimes we'd just take our food with us. We'd have a snack at nine. We'd take what they called a bait – elevenses – as they used to call it. We'd eat lunch together and we'd all be laughing about different things – what was on the wireless or what was on the telly. Some of them would say, 'You're not old enough, get on with your work, boy, you shouldn't know things about that.' The old men used to suck their old clay pipes. 'Carry on,' they'd say, 'carry on.' I learned a lot from those men. We'd come home for our real dinner and then come home again at five. You'd finish for the day and you'd have to be ready the next morning at seven o'clock.

I used a horse on a farm for mucking out pigs. That's why I like horses now. They're a good friend, a horse was. It's not like getting on a tractor and putting it in gear. You'd just say, 'Gee up!' and it would go forward without you. You know, the horse would just sidle up to the next heap wherever you wanted it to go. They were lovely things. They'd go where a tractor wouldn't go. A tractor would get stuck in a field, but a horse wouldn't. They were Suffolk horses – they were the best ones to use. The other ones were all right, but the Suffolk punches knew what they'd got to do. Once you'd got a horse walking the furrow that'd keep him there.

It took a long time for me to learn to harness a horse, but I could do that. You had to. Farmer used to say, 'We'll muck the pigs out today. Go get the horse up.' I knew what that meant. It was easy to get up near a shed with a horse. They were small.

With a tractor and trailer you need such a big area to move about, but with a horse you could just back up anywhere and just muck out with them, you know. We'd work with a muck fork. We didn't worry about the smell. We got used to it and came home smelling terrible.

I had a favourite horse. Valley I used to call it, a mare, about twenty years old, lovely old mare, you could do anything with it. When I used to go get it off the meadow I would lead it back to the gate by the hair. It never stamped its feet, never had a temper. It stood there, looking just beautiful.

After I retired, I went around the farms and helped people out the odd time and then I went round the village helping people out with their own gardens. And the churchyard. One day I'll go up to the churchyard with the mower and the next day I go all around the stones with the strimmer. You've got to have a strimmer in a churchyard, that's the main thing. That give it that finish and make it look nice.

I don't know who would keep the churchyard looking nice if I didn't. Another chap used to do it, but he packed up for one reason or another. Then they asked me to do it, and I've been doing it two years now. I don't charge nothing for it. Years ago I used to keep the churchyard looking nice, when we first lived about here, so I knew where all the paths were. They all got grown over with grass. I dug them out and put a path in. It was something to do. They asked me if I wanted to take care of the churchyard because I like grass cutting. It's a job. It'll keep you fit, won't it? When I weren't doing them jobs in people's gardens I could do the churchyard.

It all keeps you occupied. Even when you're retired you ain't finished then. You still have to keep it going, haven't you? I don't sit about. When you've got a bad back they say you've got to lie on a board or on a bed, but that's wrong. You get a bad back and you still got to keep on the move, or you'll get set fast.

You have to keep going, keep helping the village, do things, have functions. We used to have fêtes and all that years ago when my sister was here. We still have the odd flower show, but things is changed now. People aren't interested. They don't feel they want to do much. I shall keep doing the churchyard. That's an interesting job and there's satisfaction when you've done it. You think, Oh well, that's something I've done for the village. If you keep doing things for the village, perhaps other people will catch on and do something too.

I check on all the old people what can hardly get about. I keep an eye out and watch them just to see if they're all right. They often ask me to do a little job for them. I'll do the job and they'll say, 'Where's he gone? I didn't see him.'

'Oh, he's gone,' someone will say to them. 'He don't want nothing, he's gone.'

You can't take nothing off old people. Maybe you could take money; I don't. They'll give me something for Christmas. But other people I do jobs for in the village, they pay me a little for what I do. I guess it's half Christian and half for the village, if you know what I mean.

We had been brought up with the church. Mother and Father, they were strict to make us go to church. I wear a cross too. Although I don't go to church now, I do believe in the church. I do go now and again to Remembrance Day and funerals. I go to all the funerals of the top church people. But mostly I'm always in the churchyard, sweeping up the leaves, sweeping the path, taking dead flowers off, hedge cutting. I don't have time to think about if the village cares for me. I just don't worry. They all speak to me, always wave when I go by. Some would say he's a fool for what he do. Others say he do well at what he do. You don't know what people say. I just satisfy myself with what I do.

The churchyard has a lot of yew trees. They say they're poisonous, but they're using them for cancer nowadays, aren't they?

There's yew trees, cherry trees, and what they call the aeroplane propeller ones. They don't like me staying up there too late in the dark because people might get worried. There's one poor old boy who just died. I used to borrow his strimmer from him. One night he come looking for me because I didn't get done till nine o'clock and it was getting dark. He wondered where I was. He must have thought I'd fallen down in there, because they'd said to me, 'You'll be back before dark with the strimmer?' They wanted to lock the shed. I said, 'Of course I will.' So the poor old boy come back to see me. I could see his shadow coming up in the distance.

I recognize the names in the churchyard. As you go past you see the same old writing and that. There is some who I've known, a lot who I've known. Then there's this old boy, the one who used to lend me the strimmer. He just died recently, at harvest festival time. I was in there yesterday, strimming. I often strim around his grave. I do miss him. I still use his strimmer, even though I've my own mower. It makes you think you don't know what's going to happen. He died suddenly, so quick. When the funeral was held the family did say how nice the churchyard looked. People say it's the best it's ever looked – but I don't like to say that, because there's other people been doing this job before me.

*Akenfield Redux*

*The phone doesn't ring all afternoon. Cars can't even get close to
Blythe's cottage. A warning sign out front reads, simply, 'Mud'.
The only sound when the conversation pauses is the hiss of the
ash burning and the stuccato plucking sounds of his cat
attacking the furniture. At the end of the afternoon he walks
with me to the bus stop, a wooden shack in front of a wide field.*

When I wrote Akenfield, I suppose I was seeing the last of all the
ordinary farm work being done. I shouldn't think there's half a
dozen people in this village of 400 now who work on the land. So
without meaning to be, the book is a period piece of village life
before the commuters and the telly and the new farming methods
all arrived. I wasn't interested in quaintness or crafts, picturesque
things necessarily. It's a slightly hard book, not sentimental. People
always say 'the good old days'. People then were extremely poor!
Their houses were uncomfortable and damp. Children left school
very early. In that village in that time it was very hard to get away,
to do anything or to be yourself, and people worked and worked
and worked until they died. Between the wars they were getting
twenty-seven and six a week, they could be given the sack any
minute, and they worked sixty to seventy hours a week on the land
and often got one day's holiday a year, Christmas Day.

Many men would be outside all day hedging and ditching. In H. Rider Haggard's farmer's diary, written in the late nineteenth century, he sees some people draining a field with branches in the winter. It was awful work, unendurably dreadful. He couldn't make out why they didn't complain. Why they didn't rebel, why they went on and on. He could see they were unhappy. He put it down as accurately as he could. He wrote a very great inventory of what was happening. It was called *Rural England* and came out in 1901. But he was mystified by the awful plodding toil. By the time I was a child a generation later, people still began working at eight and ten years of age, doing some job or another as well as going to school. Humping the great big sacks on to carts – they ruined their backs sometimes. The physical toil was enormous; there was no machinery. Digging a ditch was absolutely dreadful.

Scandal and nosiness were oppressive things. You couldn't do anything without being noticed. You certainly couldn't live with somebody. People would look through the curtains when they hung the washing out. When that one neighbour got back late on Sunday, where had he been? All this was of enormous interest to everybody, it was a kind of endless observation. It used to be that the parish pump was where everybody gathered to talk, kind of gossip, really. There was an awful viciousness at times. It could be persecution. People who were a bit different would leave, or just disappear after a while and go somewhere else. Until thirty years ago a rural village could be a very difficult place to live for some people.

No, there's not a lot to envy about the old days. But something has been lost. People took immense pride in their crafts, laying hedges, ploughing itself. Now a young chap comes with a plough with I don't know how many shares – twelve on either side? – and he goes up and down for a couple of days, and a vast field that would have taken him a month to do is done. In autumn he comes along again and cuts it all, all by himself.

There's a great loss too of the old festivity which you see in Hardy, of going into the harvest field when everybody had to help to get it in. It was hard work but people would be sitting in the hedges eating meals and children played and dogs ran about after rabbits. People used to shout when I was a boy, 'They're cutting at Cardy's! They're cutting at Smith's!' We went over on our bikes. There were ever so many people in the field and they went round and round until the last little disc of corn, when all the hares and rabbits ran out and were killed with sticks and dogs and taken home to be eaten. Harvest has taken on a different meaning. For generations it was the height of the year. It was symbolic to the most astonishing degree in August and September to cut the fields and put it in barns. There's very little sense of that agricultural celebration in the village any more. There's celebration of Christmas, which has become . . . I don't know, a celebration of buying? The celebration of harvest is lost, as is the May time, which was such an important part of country life, when the warm weather came and there was a little break between the hard work of sowing in the spring and the hay harvest. People cut the grass, but you can hardly call it a hay harvest like it used to be.

And people don't look at the fields now. It's a very beautiful place but you hardly ever see anyone just looking at anything. They do other things – they drive off to football matches 100 miles away, they go abroad for holidays. It's just modern life. Nor do they know much about what's growing. Some people now live in the middle of a village but seem to take no part in it. They're living urban lives in the countryside – not just here, but all over the place. Because, after all is said and done, the same television programmes, same newscasters, same everything are seen by everyone in Britain, every night, from the Orkneys to Cornwall. Most people live in identical places with fitted carpets and all the latest gadgets. It is the normality of the new comfort.

I think there's also a sense of loss in villages like this one that isn't articulated. To some, it's a good loss, good riddance. Others don't know how to frame it in words. I take their funerals sometimes. I took one of the bell ringers' mother's funeral not too long ago and a whole village came out. Not any of the 'new people', as they call them. The remnants of all the people who have been here for ever. And for a little while in the service with the hymns and what I read to them, they are all as they were long ago. Yet I know perfectly well they're going to Ipswich the next day or having the telly on. Of course they are. But for that time it is very moving.

We're seeing the last of the people who were domestic servants and farm workers. The squire, who died a few weeks ago, an old Etonian and a dear sweet man, was an old friend of mine. He didn't belong to this time at all. He belonged to a long, long time ago. He was seventy-eight. When this last generation is gone there will be a break from people who have had any experience with this life. It will be missed. Some of it will be missed: the part that cannot be put into words.

## ACKNOWLEDGEMENTS

Thank you to all those who invited me into their homes, their tractors and their places of work. Thanks to all the villagers who spoke with such eloquence and were patient when I explained that we'd have to start over because I forgot to plug in the microphone.

A large thank you to Ronald Blythe for his assistance, his patience and his correspondence, to Matt Weiland for his unerring sense of architecture, and to Ian Jack and the rest of the staff at Granta. To Lesley Levene for her helpful comments. To Maggie and Brian for the room among the chickens. To Euan Thorneycroft and my family, Marian, Clare and Scott, who sometimes wondered where, exactly, I was calling from.

Two of the interviewees, Freddie King and Charles Leverett, died in the months after my stay in Akenfield. Freddie is buried in the churchyard and has the image of two hunting dogs engraved on the top corner of his headstone. Charles, true to his word, was cremated and his ashes were placed next to those of his wife. About twenty villagers gathered at a nearby pub with his pleasantly bewildered and, she had thought, long-forgotten niece; she had just inherited his estate. Always a planner, Charles had put aside money for sandwiches and a few drinks. 'Nothing too fancy,' said one person who was there. 'Just a pleasant way to be remembered.'

# APPENDIX
## ARTHUR PECK'S ORCHARD LISTS

Early Rivers    King Dawsons
  Laxton.    September Bell
Czar    Black Bullace.
Victoria    White Bullace.
Monarch    Mary Weather Damson.
Yellow Perserve   Warick Shire Droopers
Purple Perserve   Peas good Non Such.
Gisborn         Mungee Seedling
Stint              Swan.
Bell de Louvain
Primate
Orange Plum.
Beleren.
Heron.
Berbank.
President.
Wyedale
Walord
Gurlew.
Orlean.
Autumn Compo.

Plums

Beaty of Bath          George Cave.
Descovery.             Ecd Star
Worcester              Wilm Cnurch
Alington               Jubalee.
Sterling Castle.       Ida Red.
Scarlet Pimpanel.      ~~Golden Deleme~~
Bramley                Ickoal, Red.
Rival                  Johns. Gold.
Newton Wonder.         Groonny Smith
Grenadier              Duke Devenshire
Emneth Early.          Crispen.
Late Prince Albert     Metro
Edward                 Queen Elesabeth
Coxer.                 Manouret
Doctor Harvey.         Sparten
Warners Kenty
E Russet
Katie
Golden Delicen
Adham Everlasting
White Transparant
Coderling

Apples

# HOPE DIES LAST

## Making a Difference in an Indifferent World

### *Studs Terkel*

The renowned oral historian Studs Terkel talks with more than fifty Americans to find out what makes these committed souls tick. They include well-known figures like economist John Kenneth Galbraith, folksinger Pete Seeger, and Brigadier General Paul Tibbets, the pilot of the plane that dropped the bomb on Hiroshima. But the book also focuses on the extraordinary lives of ordinary citizens. Throughout, Terkel encourages them to speak passionately and candidly on their life's work, and to muse on fundamental questions: Where does hope spring from? How can hope sustain us? How does one instill hope in others?

'Inspiring and timely . . . It is not just a social document, not just fascinating American history, but a coach's manual, complete with a number of model pep talks that may get you out of your armchair' Margaret Atwood

'If you're looking for a reason to act and dream again, you'll find it in the pages of this book' *Chicago Tribune*

'There is no one in the world who can listen like Studs Terkel' Oliver Sacks

# AND THEY ALL SANG

## The Great Musicians of the 20th Century Talk about their Music

### *Studs Terkel*

Throughout the second half of the twentieth century, Pulitzer Prize-winning oral historian Studs Terkel hosted a legendary daily radio programme in Chicago, presenting listeners with his singular take on an eclectic range of music from classical, opera and jazz to gospel, blues, folk and rock. *And They All Sang* features more than forty of Terkel's inimitable conversations from the programme with some of the greatest musicians of the past century.

'Terkel's riffs with musos from opera singers such as Gobbi and Schwarzkopf, to folk and blues luminaries such as Dylan and Joplin, by way of the composers Bernstein and Copland, and Louis Armstrong and Keith Jarrett, are a musical education'
*The Times*

'The stories spread themselves out on the page, like late-night conversations in a Chicago bar . . . The reader is left with the feeling that he is getting the subjects in the raw, hair and guard down, having a great time just being themselves' *Guardian*

# STET

## An Editor's Life

### *Diana Athill*

For nearly five decades Diana Athill helped shape some of the finest books in modern literature. She edited (and nursed and coerced and coaxed) some of the most celebrated writers in the English language, including V. S. Naipaul, Jean Rhys, Norman Mailer and Brian Moore. This candid and truthful memoir writes 'stet' against the pleasures, intrigues and complexities of her life spent among authors and manuscripts.

'A little gem . . . nostalgic, funny and valuable, written
unashamedly for those who care about books'
*Observer*

'This is a memoir of a life in publishing, and is written
with a lovely and elegant lucidity' *Daily Telegraph*

'A narrative in which the passing literary stars take
second place to an extraordinary guiding intelligence –
sceptical, amused, humane' *New Statesman*

# MY LIFE IN ORANGE

*Tim Guest*

'In 1980, at the age of six, Tim Guest was taken by his mother to spend his childhood in various communes of the Indian guru Bhagwan Rajneesh. This calm, meditative, and lyrical memoir is a testament to his recovery. Impressively, he is able to convey the spiritual longings and the political aspirations that impelled his mother and many other adults to risk so much in their quest for enlightenment and growth' Elaine Showalter, *Guardian*

'Tim Guest's extraordinary account of his childhood in the communes of Bhagwan, the notorious Indian guru, is a survivor's tale, poignant, funny and wise' Christopher Hart, *Sunday Times*

'This is the story of a very odd childhood. It is funny, gently ironic, closely observed, poignant and moving. Guest makes an astonishingly mature debut and has the rare ability to describe childhood as a small child lives it; accepting, helpless, curious. From his Life in Orange a very good writer has emerged. More will come, in whatever shade' Montagu Curzon, *Spectator*

# THE SMOKING DIARIES

## *Simon Gray*

When he turned sixty-five, the playwright Simon Gray began to keep a diary: not a careful honing of the day's events with a view to posterity but an account of his thoughts as he had them, honestly, turbulently, digressively expressed. *The Smoking Diaries* is the result.

'A moving, wildly entertaining classic of the memoirist's art, and one I can't recommend too highly'
Charles Spencer, *Sunday Telegraph*

'Has a man ever written such sustained and hilarious diatribes against himself? His latest volume of diaries is a ramble – mad, maudlin, cross, nostalgic, despairing, and very, very funny'  Craig Brown, *Mail on Sunday*

'Simon Gray's *The Smoking Diaries* is one of the funniest books I have ever read in my life'  Philip Hensher, *Spectator*

'Thrilling . . . I'm a besotted fan'  Lynn Barber, *Observer*